ISBN 978-0-265-60000-9
PIBN 10873614

SOME EARLY RECORDS AND DOCUMENTS OF AND RELATING TO THE TOWN OF WINDSOR CONNECTICUT 1639-1703

HARTFORD
CONNECTICUT HISTORICAL SOCIETY
1930

The documents here printed are among the earliest records of one of the three towns which united to form the Colony of Connecticut. That the most extended of these documents is a private record and that some of the others can hardly be designated as official records, does not lessen their interest or value. Families whose descendants are now to be found in all parts of the country, are here set down with the utmost care; the names of those who had civil rights in the young colony are given; the method of governing the new town is shown; ecclesiastical controversies are touched upon, and the taxable worldly goods of each inhabitant, with their values, are recorded.

All of these original documents have been in the possession of the Connecticut Historical Society for more than three-quarters of a century.

The data contained in the Matthew Grant record was printed in part in the "New England Historic Genealogical Register" in 1851 and was incorporated by Henry R. Stiles, M. D., into his "History of Ancient Windsor," the first edition of which was published in 1859. There is reason for believing that in compiling this work, Dr. Stiles did not compare the copy which he used with the original record. In 1905 the writer of this note made a careful copy of the record, which has been used in the present printing, and the "printer's proof" of which has been twice read with the original manuscript. The whole record is now for the first time printed all together in its original form.

Since the Matthew Grant record was here put in type, comparison has been made with another early copy, which is found to contain a few names and dates now missing in the original record and not appearing in the early copies which had been previously consulted.

In order to include these names and dates in this publication, a number of lines have been reprinted as an appendix. As there are numerous manifest errors in this copy, it is possible that caution should be used in accepting these additions. Dates now missing from the original record have also been supplied from entries made by Matthew Grant himself on the early land records of the Colony, now in the office of the Secretary of the State at Hartford. This material was published in 1898 by Edwin Stanley Welles with the title "Births Marriages and Deaths returned from Hartford, Windsor and Fairfield."

A. C .B.

CONTENTS

THE

MATTHEW GRANT RECORD

USUALLY CALLED THE

OLD CHURCH RECORD

1639-1681

WITH ADDITIONS

1685–1696

1717–1740

The Matthew Grant "Old Church Record" of Windsor, so called, now in possession of the Connecticut Historical Society, remains in the paste board box in which it has been kept since its receipt by the Society in 1853. The box, now somewhat delapidated, measures 7 x 9½ x 2¾ inches, is covered with light blue paper, and on its cover is written the following probably in the hand of Dr. Sill:

"An Ancient Manuscript relating to the early Settlement of Windsor Conn Containing Births Deaths Marriages &c &c &c Deposited by Theodore Sill M. D. of Windsor Ct. Jany 1st 1853 & subject to his order Found among the Papers of the late Revr^{d} Henry A. Rowland for 40 years Pastor of the Congregational Church in Windsor

"A Copy of this Manuscript is deposited in the Town Clerks Office at Windsor Conn."

On a corner of the cover Rev. Thomas Robbins, the librarian of the Society for many years, has written, "From Dr. Theodore Sill, Windsor."

A copy made by Colonel James Loomis of Windsor as early as 1850 contains the following history of the manuscript, written by Deacon Jabez Haskell Hayden, Windsor's able historian.

"It doubtless remained his private property and in his family. There appears no evidence that it was ever passed over to the town authorities, or ever became a part of the church records. Samuel Grant, eldest son of Matthew, was among the early settlers on the east side of the river, and his descendants continued to go east as far as Ellington, and it is strong presumptive proof that this record was held in Ellington as late as 1740 when this list of deaths from 1717 to 1740 was entered, more than half a century after the death of Matthew Grant. In 1767 (?) Peletiah Birge of Windsor married Mary Grant of

Ellington, and brought his bride to the Birge Homestead, (then standing on the site of the late Roswell Miller House). After remaining there a short time they removed to Windsor Locks. About the year 1800 the Birge Homestead, then known as the Molly Birge House, was pulled down, and Oliver Ellsworth Jr. in searching among the ruins discovered this manuscript book. How came it in the Birge family? Presumably Peletiah's bride Mary Grant of Ellington brought it to Windsor, and left it at the Birge homestead, when she went to live at Pinemeadow, Windsor Locks. Fortunately the young man who found it was able to appreciate its value, and carried it to his father Chief Justice Ellsworth, who gave it to Pastor Rowland. At his death (1835) it passed into the hands of his son in law Theodore Sill, then to Col Loomis about 1840, where I found it and held it long enough to make a copy for myself, and this copy was made from mine. There is also an earlier copy made by one of the Rev. Mr. Rowlands sons, which has since come to light, and is now in the Town Clerks office in Windsor."

The manuscript itself now consists of 48 leaves measuring about 6 x 7¾ inches. With the exception of two leaves of records now loose from the others, and some occasional scribbling by later hands it is almost entirely in the handwriting of Matthew Grant. It seems to be made up of two parts or signatures. The first part comprising 14 leaves, seven on each side of the fold. The first six are now represented only by fragmentary stubs, some of them about one and one half inches in length, which bear no trace of writing. The seventh is fragmentary and is torn from the book, and the records upon it are in a black ink such as was used by Grant in writing the later portions of the record. The records proper seem to begin on the eighth leaf, and it is possible that the previous leaves were originally folded back so as to form the end of the manuscript; the absence of a cover making this possible. The reverse of the fourteenth leaf is only partly filled with records.

The second part consists of 38 leaves, 19 on each side of the fold. The first leaf, except for scribbling upon it, is blank. The record begins on the obverse of the second leaf. Two loose leaves contain entries in a different hand and of a later date. The water stains on these two leaves are identical with those on the last leaf of this second part, apparently showing that they originally belonged at this end.

It is possible that the two parts were originally two distinct and separate records, and were sewed together to form one volume by Grant himself during the years when he was making out this copy. For it must be remembered that this record is only a copy begun by Grant in 1674 from an old book then full.

The paper forming the volume is very brown and is now exceedingly brittle. Many of the edges have become broken off or have worn away. The ink in some places is very faint and almost the color of the paper. The writing is old fashioned and often difficult to read.

Missing portions of the record are indicated by the insertion of brackets. Words or letters which appear in copies made more than seventy-five years ago; but which are now missing, due to the crumbling of the paper, are inserted within the brackets. Other words or letters which are not found in the early copies; but have been supplied from the general context, are further enclosed by parentheses within the brackets. The pagination has been added in brackets.

[13
[ ] bought windſor [
[ ]er to ſet down parſ[
[ ]y, ſuch in full com[

John[ ]
Thom[ ]
Nath[ ]
Rich[ ]
[ ]
william fille
Samuell fille
Nathanel cook
corn[(e)]l[(iu)]s g[(i)]llet
Jonathan Gillet
nathan Gillet
william Phelps
Peter Brown
Robu[(d H)]ayward

mr chancy
mr Pinne
John Gaylr snr
Walter gaylr
Samuell Gaylar
Timoty Buckland
Samuell forward
gorg Phelps
Mathew Grant
Thomas Deble
Stepen Taylar
Samuell Rockwell
Samuell Baker
nathanell Biſſell

[
r[
Ab[

Adult parſons on liſt
Thomas Allyn
owen Tudor
Joſep loomys
[ ] ſonn Joſep
John Porter snr[1]
his ſonn John
Joſep lomis of J.
John moor
Samuel Biſell

Timothy Phelps
Samuel wilſon
nicolas Senchon
Thomas barber

Joſias eleſwort
John Gaylar iunr
Joſep Phelps

---

1 Probably snr, possibly inr

John Higle
Jofep Skiner
John Drak sn^r
John Drak iun^r
Job Drak of John
Jofep Baker
Samuell Barbr
John Saxfton
[ ] Sanders
[ ]ep[ ]illet
[ ]t

John Phelps
Thomas Bifell
Samuell Grant
Tahan Grant
John grant
Thomas Deble iun^r
John Strong
Return Strong
Samuell Gibbes

[14]
[ ]
[ ]ne dead his Cloth[[1]]
[ ]t his bowells lay [ ]
[ ] a fmall mater . an[ ]
[ ] goe theather and h[ ]
[ ] 12 men for a Jury [ ]
[ ] John loomys . John [ ]
[ ]e . Samuell biffell . Jo[ ]
[ ] leftenant ffylar . Th[ ]m[ ]
[ ], Jacob gibbes . Samuell gib[ ]
[ ] his hows and fawe him . and thay w[ ]
[ ]thes by m^r wolcott to giue thire a[ ]
[ ]e caues of his death . and this was the [ ]
[ ] that there was an emmynent [ ]
[ ] fat by ye fyer he fell into a found [ ]
[ ] hayer his belly before ye fyer his f[ ]

1 This page is so much worn that it can only be read with difficulty

[ ]me . his heed at ye fouth game[1] . his clo[ ]
[ ] burnt his flefh wonderfully . and th[ ]
[ ]ome hard no noyes from him .

[15] math[(ew Gra)nt [ ] Church [thin]gs in feuerall p[]ickla[(rs since our)] firft fetting downe here in Windfor, at leaft [(since Mr)] Hewits firft coming up here vnto us . Aguft . [(1639)] And becauf the elders of the Church haue [(a record)] of Church pcedings in fume things as thay [ ] wich[2] thay had, therefore in fuch things as [(there)] be to fpeake to I fhall fett down here in [the (ord)]er I can . Conferning the admifsion of pe[r(fons to)] full communion . I could giue a count of [(all but)] Judg there is no need of fuch as are dead . and [ ] gonn from us to other places . and for children that haue bin baptifed . tha[(t rem)]aine with us, I fhall name in their order, and [ ]

And other that haue not made out for full co[m(munion)] onely to attaine baptifme for thire childr[en]

[4]I here not dune conferning br . liftenant wi[l(ton)] did remoue from Windfo Church to goe to no[rth(ampton)] to help to firther a Church thear . ye beginn[ing] march 25 . and now febury ye 6 . 1677 . he wa[s b(uried)] here in Windfor , he dyed ye day before:

[16 (A Lift of thofe members of the church that) were so in] Do[r-chester a]nd ca[me up here] with mr [(Wareham)and ftill ar]e of us .

[(of men)]	of women
[(Henry Wolc)]ott	mftrs Phelps

1 Possibly carne[r]
2 This word is crossed out in the original
4 The remainder of the page is in black ink

[(William P)h]elps
[(John Witc)h]feld
[(William G)]aylard
[(John M)]oore
[(Thomas)f]ford
[(Humphrey Pinn)]e
[(Walter)fi]llar
[(Mathew)] Grant
[(Thomas)] Deble sen^{r}
[(George)Ph]illups
[(Jonathan)] Gillet sen^{r}
[(Nathan G)]illet
[(Richard Vore)]
[(Abram R)and]all
[(Begat Egg)e]lſton
[(George Phe)]lps

[(Men tha)t] ha[u] ben taken
[(into)] communion ſinc we
[(cam)e h]ere, I ſet them down
[(acc)ord]ing to ye yeare and
[(da)y of] ye month thay ware
[(ad)mi]tted and now remaine.

[(Wi)]lliam Phelps. noum . 17 . 39 .
[(Joh)]n Biſsell senr . may . 3 . 1640 .
[(John)] Loomys . octo^{r} . 11 . 1640 .
[(Bene)dicts] Aluard . octo . 17 . 1641 .
[(Robard)Hay]ward . July . 10 . 42 .
[(Daniel) Clark] . June . 18 . 1643 .

Decon moors Wife
Ric . Vors Wife
Jonath . Gillets Wife
liftn . fillers Wife
Tho . Debls Wife
georg Phelps Wif

Womin admited here

Mst Pinne . febu[ry] . 9 . 1639 .
ould wido Drake . feb . 23 . 39 .
Mst Wolcot . Aprell . 26 . 1640 .
Sam . gaylars wife Apl . 27 . 45 .
Abr . Randals Wife . Aguſt . 17 . 45 .
Bene Aluards Wife . Janu^{r}. 13 . 47 .
the Wido . Hoſkins . Apel . 9 . 48 .
ould mst Allyn . Aguſt . 5 . 1649 .
nicolas Senchons Wife Jan^{r} 22 . 49 .
Will . fillys wife . July . 17 . 1651 .
nat . Cooks Wife . aguſt . 29 . 52 .
William Phelps Wife . mar . 11 . 54 .
Mst . Newbery . Aprell . 1 . 1655 .
ye wife of John Loomys [ ] . 55 .
ye wife of John Drak [ ]8 . 55 .
ye wife of m^{r} . D. Clark . [ ] . 11 . 58.
ye wife of Thomas ford[ ] . 30 . 60.

[(Stephen Ta)ylar] . march . 31 . 44 .
[ ]
[ ]

ye wife of Joſe loom[ys] . 25 [ ]
ye [wif]e of water [(Gaylar)]

[17] of [men]
Robart W[at]ſon . Janur . 22 . 49 .
Walter Gaylar . may . 5 . 51 .

John moore ordayned
Deacon . Janur . 11 . 1651 .

John Rockwell . July . 31 . 53 .
captn Newbery . Apl . 11 . 1658 .
Jacob Drak . Apl . 11 . 1658
Samuell Rockwel
& Jonā . gillet both . Apl . 6 . 1662 .
Peter brown and Nathanel
Cooke both . June . 22 . 1662 .
Samuell loomys . noumr . 26 . 1661 .
Samuel Marſhall . may . 3 . 1663 .
Nathanell loomys . may . 3 . 63 .
Cornelus Gillet &
timthy Bukland . Janur . 16 . 1665 .
John Gaylar & Thomas
loomys taken in Apell . 3 . 66 .
John madeſly . octobr . 7 . 1666 .
Iſack Phelps . Janury . 27 . 1666 .
mr Nathanell chancy made
publick declaration of his faith
in chriſtian princples, & the

[(of women)]
ye wife of Samuel loomys . [ ]
ye wife of JohnPorter . may. 3[(63)]
ye wife of Henry denſlo. Apl . [(65)]
Thomas Allyns Wife &
return Strongs Wife &
TimothyBucklands wife. Janr[(65)]
Henery Wolcots wife
John moors wife &
Thomas loomys wife . Aprel . [(66)]
Jacob draks wife June . 3 . [(66)]
Stephen Taylars Wife . Agu [(66)]
John Strongs wife &
ſhee was baptiſed . Aguſ[(66)]
Joſias eleſwort Wife &
Samuel Gibbſs wife . ſept . [(66)]
Samuel Bakrs wife . octo . 2[(70)]
Samul fillys wife . decmb . [(70)]
mary Saxſton& baptiſed[(Apr 71)]
ye wido fox . Jun[ ]
nathanl Winchls wife . Ag[(71)]
cornelus gillets Wife . f[(eb 71)]
ye wife of Nathane[ll]
loomas ſeptm . 28 . 7[(3)]
elizabeth chapman
wido taken in to church

maner of gods working one
his fowle . Janury . 12 . 1667 .

communion . Aprel . 22 . 167[(3)]

———

Samuell filly taken into
full communion . decemb . 18 . 70 .
Samuell fforward . octo . 8 . 71 .
Samuell Baker . Aprell . 7 . 1672 .
Timothy Hall . Aprell . 28 . 72 .
Nathanell Bifsell
mr chancy reding what
he tok from priuat
feptem . 28 . 73 .
william filly taken into
church comunion . march . 8 . 1673 .
Samuell gaylar taken into
church[1] comunion . Juen . 28 . 1674 .

[18 Blank page.]

[19] A full and clear copy of this book may be seen in the town clerks office at Windsor (1854 .)[2]

[20] John Eliot
His Book[3]

[21] June . 21 . 1668 . It was by a vote of the Church afsented to, t[hat] Adult pfons , be it hufban or wife, that defired to have th[eir] children Baptifed by mr Chancy, fhould, if thay prefent[ed] them felues to the

1 This word is almost illegible.
2 A modern entry in pencil.
3 Handwriting unidentified; written later than the record itself.

Elders in ꝑiuat, and declared to the[ir] fateſfaction, thire knowledg in the princples & owned th[e(ir)] fathers couinant, then there ſhould nothing be required of t[hem] in publick, vtill thay preſented them ſelues for full c[om]munion .
before this time it had bin the practic to call ſuch ꝑſons in publiqu to ſtand forth and anſwer to queſtions of catte[chism] propounded to them . & to owne ye church couinant .
And the time which mr warham firſt begann this ꝑactice was . January . 31 . 1657 . and went owne in the practic of [it] vntill . march . 19 . 1664 . which day he declared t[o the] church that he had meet with ſuch arguments againe[st the] practic conferning the baptiſing of members child[ ]ldren, that he could not get throw at ꝑeſent, & cou[ld not] goe one in ꝑactic as hee had don . without ſcrupiel of conſcienc, therfore muſt for bare untill he had way[ed ar]guments and aduiſed with thoſe that ware able to giue . not that he intinded to caſt of ye practtic holy, but onely laye it for a time till he could be better able to anſw[er] his preſent ſcruples . for if he ſhould act, and not o[f] faith . rom . 14 . would be ſin to him .
ſo the delaye of it from . mach . 19 . 64 . was three years and [ſo] much as from the . 19 of march to the 21 of Juen, that m[r] Chancy ſett it one agayne .

[1]febuary . 16 . 78 . Joſcp ſkiner hauing neuer bin baptiſed deſired that he might be baptiſed and ye church granted it ſo he would be tried conferning his noledg and blamles life . and one ye church couinant and come under diſſaplin . to be oned as a Sub[2] me[m-] ber . and ſo any others might come in in lick maner . me[n] or women kind . [3]one ye 2 of march . ther was non that la[y] any blame

1 Beginning here the remainder of the page is written in black ink.

2 The last letter of the word is blotted and uncertain.

3 The sentence beginning here is in black ink, but appears to have been written at a different time from that which preceeds it.

on him in point of his conuerſation, ſo he ond ye c[hurch] couinant and was baptiſed,

[22 Blank page.]

[23] here I note down the parſons in order as thay tendr[ed] them ſelues publickly, to attayn baptiſme for thire child[ren] (from the time mr Warham firſt begann untill he layed [(it)] downe) and remayne ſo ſtill and haue not put one for full communion . nor haue not Joyned them ſelues with the other company,

Thomas Biſsell
Mary Marſhall
Wife of Nathanel
Biſsell[1] loomys .
theſe . Janury . 31 . 57 .

febury . 28 . 57 .
Samuell Gaylar
Wife of John gaylar
Wife of Thomas Biſsell

may . 22 . 59 . ſamuell grant
July . 17 . 59 . Peter browns Wife

noumr . 27 . 59 . John Biſsell .
& ſamuell Biſsell .

noumbr . 8 . 63 . Timothy Phelps

Sinc mr chancy begann as I can
Judg by his baptiſing thir childr[en]
Wife of Timothy Hall . July . 5 . 68 .
Dauid Winchell
& Iſrel Deble . ſeptm . 18 . 70 .
Joſep Gaylar . July . 16 . 71 .
Samuel Barbar . octo . 12 . 71
Surroball ffylar . march . 6 . 69 .
Samuell Deble octobr . 2 . 1670
John grant octo . 22 . 71 .
Jonathan Winchel . feb . 67 .
John Portr iun febu . 7 . 1670 .[2]
nicolas Buckland march . 16 . 72 .
Iſrell Debel Wif octo [(6)] . 7 [(2)]

1 This word is crossed out.
2 The year appears to have been first written 1670 and changed to 1671.

decmb^{r} . 27 . 63 . wife of Tahan Grant

decmb^{r} . 11 . 64 . ebenzr Deble .

march . 12 . 64 . Return Strong .
& Samuell Gibbes .

[24 Blank page.]

[25] Here I ſet down ye names and ages of perſons both of [(men and)] women kind that haue ben borne and baptiſed in Windſor chur[ch] and are yet vnmarried and not of thoſe that have turned to [the] other ſoſiety . but liue ſtill under ye churches cognicenc .

men kind	women kind
Stephen Taylar . march . 16 . 44 .	meriam Deble . Deſim . 7 . 45 .
Thomas egelſton . noum . 22 . 46 .	Sara Pinne . Decm . 3 . 48 .
Joſep Phelps . July . 11 . 47 .	Sara buckland . Apel . 1 . 49 .
Thomas Debel . ſeptm . 3 . 47 .	Sara wolcot . July . 8 . 49 .
Samuel Wolcot . aprel . 15 . 56 .	eliſubth Aluard . ſept . 21 . 51 .
Jeremy gillet . feb . 20 . 47 .	mary wolcot . decm . 7 . 51 .
John gaylar . febr . 4 . 48 .	Sara gailr . Janur . 18 . 51 .
Joſias Aluard . July . 8 . 49 .	Hanna fille . July . 3 . 53 .
John Birg . Janur . 20 . 49 .	Abigail of ſamuel
Joſias gillet . July . 14 . 50 .	gaylar baptiſd . oct . 1 . 53 .
Thomas Buckland . feb . 9 . 50 .	ruth Rockwell . marc . 11 . 54
John lomis of Jiſep . octo . 5 . 51	Sara Rockwel born . may . 12 . 5[ ]
Joſep Birg . noum^{r} . 2 . 51 .	Hana of John Drak
John Taylar . marc . 28 . 52 .	born . aguſt 8 . 53 bap[tised]
John Drak born . ſept . 14 . 49 .	aprel . 15 . 55 .
baptiſed . Apel . 15 . 55 .	rebeca nubery . may . 6 . 53

Job Drak born Juen . 15 . 51 .
baptifed apel . 15 . 55 .
beniamn gaylar . Apl . 15 . 55 .
epharim Hayward . Janr . 11 . 56 .
Danel lomys of iohn . Juen . 21 . 57.
Thomas lomys of Tho .
lomas borne . mar . 17 . 55 .
baptifed . febr . 7 . 57 .
Samuel marfhal born . may . 27 . 53
baptifed febury . 7 . 57 .
nathanel loomys of nath baptifd . feb . 7 . 57 .
Thomas bifsell born . octo . 2 . 56 .
baptifed . febury . 7 . 57 .
Jofia elefwort baptifd . mar . 7 . 57 .
Jofia wolcot . July . 25 . 58 .
Samuell Grant . may . 22 . 59 .
[S]imon Drak of John . octor . 30 . 59 .

ledia marfhal born . feb . 18 [ ]
baptifed . febary . 7 . 57 .
Hana loomys of T. baptifd . feb . 14 . [ ]
elifabet Elfwort . marh . 7 . 5[ ]
abigayl Taylar . mar . 28 . 5[ ]
mary clark . feptmr . 26 . 5[ ]
martha Gaylar . June . 24 . 6[ ]
mary ftrong . Aprell . 25 . 5[8]
hanna ftrong . feptmr . 2 . 60 .
mary Brown . July . 24 . 59 .
Hanna Brown . feptmr . 30 . 60 .
abigayl Brown . Auft . 10 . 62 -
Hepfiba Brown . noumr . 20 . 6[ ]
mary Bifsel of John . Dcmr . 4 . [ ]
Ruth of John Drak . Decmr [ ]

[26] [m]en kind
John Bifsell of famuell
born . Apell . 5 . 59 .
baptifed . noumbr . 27 . 59 .
John Bifsell of Thoms . Janr . 27 . 60.
Jofia lomys of nathã . febr . 24 . 60 .

Robart Watfon was taken into church fellowfhip in . 49 . and may 11 . 51 . he was caft out and fo ftod till January . 18 . 56 . betwixt

lidia of John Drak . feb . 2 . 61 .

---

ye wife of John Porter
admited to church fellofhip
may . 3 . 63 . & had 6 cheldren
baptifed . John 12 yers of Age
mary . 10 yers . Sara . 8 yers
James . 6 yers . nathanell . 3 yer
Hanna 5 mouthes . may . 10 . 63 .
Samuell Porter . mar . 12 . 64 .

his caſting out & taking in he
had mary . John . & Samuell .
which 3 children ware baptiſd
[J]anuary . 25 . 56 .
his dafter Hanna . Aguſt . 15 . 58.
ebenezr Watſon . Apel . 28 . 61 .
nathanl Watſon . Janury . 30 . 63 .
Jededia Watſon . octo . 7 . 66 .

[Jo]hn Biſsell of John . may. 12 .61.

[Th]e wife of ouen Tudor
[t]aken into church felloſhip
[A]prel . 28 . 61 . and then ſhee
[had] fiue children baptiſed
[S]amuell . owen . fara . Jane .
mary . may . 12 . 61 .

---

enock Drak . Decmb[r] . 10 . 55 .
Thomas Allyn . marc . 15 . 62 .
[E]leezor gaylar . mac . 15 . 62 .
Joſeph of Tho . Biſsel . Apl . 19 . 63.
Timothy of timoty Phelpes
baptiſed . noumbr . 8 . 63 .
Thomas Taylar , octo . 12 . 55 .
mathew of Joſep lomys . noū . 6 . 64.
nathanell cook . may . 16 . 58 .
John cooke . Aguſt . 10 . 62 .
Joſia cooke . deſm . 25 . 64 .

Rebeca Porter . mar . 10 . 66 .
Heſter Porter . may . 9 . 69 .
ruth Porter . Aguſt . 20 . 71 . m[r] chancy

---

mary Taylar . June . 23 . 61 .
mindwell Taylar . noum . 8 . 63 .
mary of fam: Rockwl . Jan[y] . 26 . 61 .
Anna of fam : fille . fept . 25 . 64 .
Hanna of Joſep lomys . feb . 8 . 61 .

Sara of nathanel cook
borne Juen . 28 . 1650 .
baptiſed . octobr . 17 . 52 .
Lidia cooke baptiſed . Janur . 17 . 52 .
hanna cooke baptisd . octo . 28 . 55 .
Abigayl cooke . march . 7 . 59 .

Mary of ebenezr Deble . born
Decm[r] . 24 . 64 : baptiſd . 25 . 64 .

Abigayl of Will . filly . aguſt 22 . 58
Debro of Will . filly . marc . 24 . 61 .

Hepſiba of Samuell gibbs
Baptiſed . march . 12 . 64 .
Patienc[1] Daftr of Sam : gibes
baptiſed deſcembr . 9 . 66 .
Eliſabet gibbs . Janury . 31 . 68 .
Joanna gibbes . Aprell . 2 . 71 .

1 Experenc was first written and crossed out.

[W]akefeld ſonn of ebenezr
[D]eble . ſeptm . 15 . 67 . baptiſed
[M]ay . 17 . 68 .
[Eben]ezr of ebenezr Debl
[baptiſ]ed . aguſt . 17 . 71 .

[27] William of will . filly
mar . 12 . 64 .
Jonathan of Jonathan gillet iunr
baptiſed . febury . 19 . 70 .
Jeremy Aluard . of . B . A .
baptiſed . Janury . 31 . 55 .
Joſias Barber . feb . 15 . 53 .
Thomas of Tim . bukland .
Jan[r] . 21 . 65 .
Joſias Clark . Janur . 28 . 48 .
Danill Clark . apel . 10 . 54 .
John Clark . apel . 15 . 56 .
Samuell Clark . July . 7 . 61 .
Sara Clark . aguſt . 9 . 63 .
Nathanel Clark . ſeptm . 9 . 66 .

Thomas eleſwort baptiſd .
ſeptm[r] . 9 . 66 .
Jonathan eleſwort . July . 4 . 69 .
John eleſwort . octobr . 15 . 71 .

Thomas fylar . march . 6 . 69 .

---

mary of Jonathan Gillet iunr
baptiſed . octo . 27[1] . 67 .

---

abigal bukland . noum . 17 . 67 .
mary bukland . noum . 17 . 7[o]

Sara of water gaylar [ ] .

Apel . 2 . 55 . ye wif of Hen[r]. Denſl[ow]
taken to church feloſhip . and had
children baptiſed . Juen . 4 . 65 .
Samuell . 6 . yer old . ruth . 12 y[ ]
abigayl . 10 . yer . Debora . 8 . yer
Hanna . 4 . yer . eliſabet bap[ ]
febuary . 18 . 65 .

Hanna Buckland . ſeptm . 18 . 54 .
ruth drak of John . deſm . 6 . 57
mary Drak of John . feb . 3 . 66 .
eliſabet Drak . July . 24 . 64[2]
mary elſwort . may . 9 . 60 .
martha eleſwort . deſem[r] . 13 . 6[2]

William fillys wif admited . Jul[y]
17 . 51 . and childrn baptiſed . ſamuel
John . mary . eliſabeth . aguſt . 3 . 5[ ]
abigayl filly . Aguſt 28 . 58 .

---

1 First written 26.
2 Part of the last figure is missing, but it apparently is a 4.

John fille born . defm . 15 . 45 .
baptifed . aguft . 3 . 51 .

Samuell of Samuel filly . Apel .
3 . 70 .
John[1] Hefecia of William
Gaylar . febury . 14 . 52 .

Samuell of Samuel gaylar . July. 57.
Ephraym Hayward . Janu^r^ . 11 . 56.
Jeremy of Tho . lomys . July .
10 . 70 .
Jonathan of N . lomys . Aprel .
3 . 64 .
Dauid of N . lomys . Janury .
12 . 67 .
Hefekia of N . lomis . feb . 28 . 68 .
mofes of N . lomis . may . 21 . 71 .
Jofep of John lomys . noum . 7 . 51 .
Thomas of John lomys . def . 3 . 53 .
Timothy of John lomys . July .
28 . 61 .
Nathanel of J lomys . 12 . 63 .
Dauid of John lomys . Juen . 4 . 65 .
Ifack of John lomis . fept . 6 . 68 .
[S]amewel lomis . aguft . 19 . 66 .

mary of famul filly Apell . 1[ ]
Abigal of famuell filly . [ ]
mary of John gaylar . Janury . 2[ ]
John of John gaylar . Juen . 25 [ ]
elifabet gaylar . febary . 26 . [ ]
lidia Hayward . June . 16 . 55
mary of Thomas[2] lomys . Jan^r^ .
17 . 5[ ]
Elifabet of Tho. lomys . Jan^r^ . 23 . 6[ ]
ruth of Tho . lomys . Apel . 8 . 66
Sara of Tho . lomys . feb . 2 . 67
Abigail of Nat . lomys . Apl . 1 . 5[ ]
Elifabet[3] . of John lomis . may . 14 . 7[ ]
mary of John loomys . aguft . 10 . 7[ ][4]
mary of John grant . may . 3 . 74 .
Jofep fon of John Drak iu^r^ . Juen .
28 . 7[ ]
Dameres dautr of R . ftrong . July .
5 . [ ]
Jofep fon . of Jofep gaylr . Aguft . [ ]

John fonn of John grant . baptifed . 62[5]
Samuel fonn of famuel gibbs . 22
baptifed Aprell . 22 . 77 .

1 This word is crossed out.
2 Jofep was first written and crossed out.
3 Timothy was first written and crossed out.
4 Beginning with this entry the records on this page seem to have been written at different times.
5 The remaining entries on this page and all on the following page are in blue ink.

[28] 29 . 77 . elifabeth chapman
had 7 children baptifed
hir fonn Henery he was Born
July . ye 4 . 1663 .
Hir . dafter . mary . was borne
octobr . 27 . 1665 .
hir dafter elizabeth Borne
Janury . 15 . 1667 .
hir fonn . fimon . Borne aprel
ye 30 . 1669 .
hir dafter Hanna Borne
may . ye . 3 . 1671 .
Hir dauter margret Born
march ye . 7 . 1672 .
Hir Daughter fara Borne
may ye . 24 . 1675 .

Elizabeth of John grant . July . 15 . 77 .

---

famuell fon of famuell Debl
baptifed . may . 13 . 77 .

---

fara dafter of John Porter iunr
baptifed . Juen . 3 . 77 .
Beniamen elfwort baptifed
aguft . 19 . 77 . born . Janury . 19 . 76 .
and ftephen of nat: winchell

---

aguft . 26 . 77 . Thomas fonn
of Thomas Debl baptifed .

ſeptm . 9 . 77 . ezecia of Iſack
phelps baptiſed ..

ſamuell ſonn of Timoty pal
mer Baptiſed . 2 decm[r] . 77 .

Thomas ſonn of Joſep ſkinr
baptiſed . 23 decm[r] . 77 .

Nathanel ſon of Timothy
Phelps baptiſed . 13 ianury . 77 .

---

elizabet dafter of ſamuell
Biſſell Baptiſed . 6 . ianury . 77 .

Thomas ſonn of Thomas New
bery . and Joſep ſonn of Iſr
ell dewey . baptiſed . 27 . Jan[r] . 77 .

John ſonn of ſamuell ſilley
baptiſed . 17 . febury . 1677 .

[29] Know all men by these presents that I
Nathaniel Taylor[1]

[30 Blank page.]

[31] May . 18 . 1674 . I here ſet down a new ye times of [(birth)]

---

1 Handwriting unidentified. Written perhaps a century later than the record itself. The name is repeated several times.

of children that has ben borne in windſor . and has come [to] my knowledg to enter them upon in ye owld Book, that being full ther is not place to ſett in order to find them .
here I enter Parſons as thay ſwet upon ye latter .
A . Benidictus Aluard married Jone nuton . noumbr . 26 . 1640 .
his ſonn Jonathan was borne . June . 1 . 1645 .
his ſonn Beniamen was born . July . 11 . 1647 .
his ſonn Joſias was Borne . July . 6 . 1649 .
his Daughter eliſabeth was Born . ſept . 21 . 1651 .
his sonn Jeremy was Borne . decembr . 24 . 55 .

Allixander Aluard . married mary Vore . octo . 29 . 1646 .
his Daughter Abigal was Borne . octobr . 6 . 1647 .
his ſonn John was Borne . Auguſt . 12 . 1649 .
his Dauter mary was Borne . July . 6 . 1651 .
his ſonn Thomas was Borne . octo . 27 . 1653 .
his Daughter eliſabeth was Born . noum^r . 12 . 1655 .
his ſonn Beniamen was Borne . febury . 11 . 1657 .
his Daughter ſara was . Borne . June . 24 . 1660 .

Georg Allixander married ſuſan . march . 18 . 1[ ]
his ſonn John was Borne . July . 25 . 1645 .
his Daughter mary was Borne . octo . 20 . 1649 .
his ſonn Daniell was Borne . Janu . 12 . 1650 .
his ſonn nathanell was Borne . Decmb . 29 . 1652 .
his Daughter ſurua was Born . Decmb . 8 . 1654 .

Thomas Allyn marryed Abigayl warram . octobr . [ ]
his ſonn John Born . Auguſt . 17 . 59 . but dyed
his ſonn mathew was Borne . Janu^r . 5 . 1660 .

his fonn Thomas was Borne . march . 11 . 62 : 63 .
his fonn famuell was Borne . noum . 3 . 67 .
his daughtr Jane was Borne . July . 22 . 70 .
his Daughter Abigal was Born . octo . 17 . 72 .
his Daughter fara was Born . July . 13 . 1674 .
his Dau[ghter] was Born . ianu[r] . 29 . 1676 .

[32] Edward Adams married elizabeth Buckland . may . 25 . 60 .
his Daughtr mary was Borne . Aguft . 28 . 1671 .

B . John Bifsell sn[r]
his fonn Nathanell was Borne in windfor, and Baptifed . fept . 27 . 40

John Bifell iun[r] . married Izrell mafon[1] . June . 17 . 1658 .
his Daughter mary was Borne . febu[r] . 22 . 1658 .
his fonn John was Borne . may . 4 . 1661 .
his fonn Danell was Borne . feptem[r] . 29 . 1663 .
his Daughter Dorety was Borne . Aguft . 10 . 1665 .
his fonn Jofias was born . in october . 10 . 1670 .
Hezecia his fonn was born Aprell . 30 . 1673
his Daughter Ann was Born aprell . 28 . 1675.
Jeremia his fonn was Born . Juen . 22 . 1677 .

[T]homas Bifsell . married Abigayl moore . octobr . 11 . 1655 .
[his] fonn Thomas was Borne . octob[r] . 2 . 1656 .
[his Dau]ghter Abigayl was Borne . noum[r] . 23 . 1658 .
[his fon] John was Borne . January . 26 . 1660 .
[his fon] Jofeph was Borne . Aprel . 18 . 1663 .
[his D]aughtr Elizabeth was Born . June 9 . 1666 .
[his f]onn Beniamen was Borne . feptm[r] . 9 . 69 .

1 He is said to have married Isabel Mason, daughter of Maj. John Mason.

[his Da]ughter fara was Borne January . 8 . 71 .
[his fo]n epram was born aprell 11 . 1676 . 11 Days aftr Died
[his Dau]ghter Efter was borne Aprell . 2 . 1677 . dyed . May . 9 . 78 .
[his fo]nn ephram bifell was born feptembr . 4 . 1680
[his fon Lu]ke was born september 22 1682[1]

[Samuel] Bifsell married Abigayl Holcom . June . 11 . 1658 .
[his fon] John was Borne . Aprell . 5 . 1659 .
[his Dau]ghter Abigayl was Born . July . 6 . 1661 .
[his fo]nn Jacob was Borne . march . 28 . 64 .
[his Da]ughter mary was Borne . feptm^r . 15 . 66 .
[his fon]n famuell was Borne . Januy . 11 . 68 .
[his fo]nn Benaga was Borne . June . 30 . 71 .
[his D]aughter Elifabeth . born . Janary . 4 . 77
[his Daught]er debora was Born . octobr . 29 . 1679 .

[33] Nathanell Bifsell . maried mindwell moors . feptm^r . 25 . [ ]
his Daughter mindwell was Borne . octo . 3 . 63 .
his fonn Nathanell was Borne . Janury . 7 . 1665 .
Jonathan his fonn . born . July . 3 . 68 . but is dead .
Hanna his Daughter was Borne . Janury . 12 . 70 .
his daughtr Abigal born . feptm^r . 14 . 73 . and dyed .
his fonn Jonathan was born . febury . 14 . 74 .
Abigal his dafter born march . 9 . baptifed ye 11 . 1676 .
Elifabeth his daughter born march ye 15 . 1679 .

Thomas Barber . married . octobr . 7 . 1640 . his wife Jane .
his fonn John was Baptifed . July . 24 . 1642 .
his fonn Thomas was Borne . July : 14 . 1644 .
his daughter fary was Baptifed . July . 19 . 46 .

1 This entry is not in Matthew Grant's handwriting.

his fonn famuell was Baptifed . octo . 1 . 1648 .
his Daughter mary was Baptifed . octo . 12 . 1651 .
his fonn Jofia was Borne . febury . 15 . 1653 .

John . Barber maried Bathfheba cogens . feptm^r . [ ]
his Daughter Joanna was Borne . Aprell . 8 . 6[7]
his fonn John was Borne . July . 14 . 1669 .

Thomas Barber married mary Phelps . Dece[ ]
his Daughtr marcy was Borne . Janury . 11 . 6[ ]
his Daughter fary was Borne . July . 2 . 1669

Samuell Barber married mary cogens . [ ]
his fonn Thomas was Borne . octobr . 7 . 1671 .
his fonn famuell was Borne . Janury . 26 . 73 .
famuell Barber maried his 2 wife ru[th Daughter]
of John Drak . Janury . 25 . 1676 .
[hi]s Daftr Hanna was Born . octobr . 4 . 16[81]

[34] Thomas Buckland decefed . I haue not ye time of his mariag
his fonn Timothy was Borne . march . 10 . 1638 .
his Daughter elizabeth was Borne . febury . 21 . 40 .
his Daughter tempranc was Born . noum^r . 27 . 42 .
his Daughter mary was Borne . octobr . 2 . 1644 . Dead
his fonn Nicolas was Borne . febury . 21 . 1646 .
his Daughter sara was Borne . march . 24 . 1648 .
his fonn Thomas was Borne . febury . 2 . 1650 . Ded[1]
his Daughter Hanna was Borne . feptm^r . 18 . 54 . Dead[1]

---

1 The Dead is crossed out and the Ded written in black ink.

Timothy Buckland married Abigall vore . march . 27 . 62 .
his ſonn Timothy was Borne . Aprell . 20 . 1664 . Dead .
his ſonn Thomas was Borne . June . 23 . 65 .
his Daughter Abigayl was Borne . noum^r^ . 11 . 67 .
his Daughter mary was Borne . noumb^r^ . 7 . 1670 .
his Daughter ſara was Borne . Aprell . 10 . 1673 .
his Daughter Hanna Born . Juen 28 . baptiſed
his daughter eliſabeth . born . July . 2 . 1676[1] .
febry . 26 . 1678[1] . July . 18 . 81 . 2 daftrs born . on . died . ye 24 day .
ye other died aguſt ye 2 day . of Nicolas buckland .

[Nicholas Bu]ckland . maried martha wackfeeld . octo . 21 . 68 .
[his ſon J]ohn was Borne . march . 13 . 1672 . Dead .
[his Daughter] Hanna was Borne . ſeptem^r^ . 1 . 1674 . Dead
[his ſon] John . born . 7 decm^r^ . dyed ye . 20 . 75 . Dead
[his Daught]er martha was borne march ye firſt . 78/77
[Two Daughter]s born . July 19 . 81 . both dead . not named

[Richard] Birg married Elizabeth Gaylar . octo^r^ . 5 . 1641 .
[his ſon] Daniell was Borne noum . 24 . 1644 .
[his Daug]hter elizabeth was Borne . July . 28 . 46 . Dead .
his ſ[onn] Jeremy was Borne . may . 6 . 1648 . Dead .
his ſ[onn] John was Borne . January . 14 . 1649 .
his ſ[onn] Joſeph was Borne . noum^r^ . 2 . 1651 .

Danel Birg maried Debra Holcom[2] . noumbr . 5 . 1668 .
His Daughtr eliſabet was Borne . Aguſt . 25 . 1670 . dead[3]

1 July 2, 1676, is probably date of baptism of Hannah, and Feb. 26, 1678, the date of the birth of Elizabeth.

2 ſara ennoo was first written and crossed out.

3 Written in black ink.

His Daughtr Debra was Borne . noum[r] . 26 . 1671 .
His Daughtr ellifabeth Born . febuary . 3 . 1674 .
[H]is fonn Danell was Born . feptem[r] . 16 . 1680 .
[Hi]s dafter mary was Born decm[r] . 25 . 1677 .

[35] Jefery Baker maried Jone Rockwell . noum . 15 . 1642 .
his fonn famuell was Borne . march . 30 . 1644 .
his Daughter Hepfiba was . Born . may . 10 . 1646 .
his Daughter mary was Borne . July . 15 . 1649 .
his Daughtr Abiell was Borne . Decm[r] . 23 . 1652 . Dead[1]
his fonn Jofeph was borne . June . 18 . 1655 .

Samuell Baker married Sara Cook . Juen . 30 . 1670 .

William Buell maried — — — — — noumb[r] . 18 . 1640 .
his fonn famuell was Borne . feptm[r] . 2 . 1641 .
his fonn Peter was Borne . aguft . 19 . 1644 .
his Daughtr mary was Borne . feptm[r] . 3 . 1642 .
his Daughtr Hanna was Born . ianury . 8 . 1646 .
his Daughtr Hepfiba . was Born . Decmb[r] . 11 . 1649 .
his Daughtr fara was Borne . march . 21 . 1653
his Dautr Abigayl was Born . febury . 12 . 165[5]

Samuell Buell married Debro Grifwold . nou[ ] . 13 . 1662
his fonn famuell was Borne . July . 20 . 1663 .

Thomas Bafcom .
his Daughtr Abigayl was Borne . June . 7 . 1640 .
his fonn Thomas was Borne . febury . 20 . 1641 .

1 Written in black ink.

his Daughter Hepſiba was Born . aprl . 14 . 1644 .

John Bartlet .
his ſonn eſaya was Borne . Juen . 13 . 1641 .
his ſonn Beniamen waſ baptiſed . marc . 26 . 43 . De[1][ ]
his Dautr Hepziba was Borne . July . 14 . 46 .
his ſonn Jehoiade . was baptiſed . Decm^{r} . 23 . 49 .
his Dauter mehetabell . baptiſed .may . 11 . 51 .

Beniamen Bartlet married . Debra Barnard . Ju[ ]
his ſonn Beniamen was Borne . June . 21 . 1668 . De[2][ ]
his dautr Debora was Borne . Aprell . 3 . 1666 .
his ſonn eſaya was Borne . Decmb^{r} . 9 . 70 .
his ſonn Abiia was Borne . July . 26 . 73 .
his ſonn Beniamen Born decmbr . 15 . 77
[36] epharem ſonn of Bengamn bartlet born . Janury . 17 . 1673 .
Jehoiade Bartlet was borne nouember . 2 . 1675 .

Ezaya Bartlet married Abia gillet . decem^{r} . 3 . 1663 .
his ſonn John was Borne . ſeptmbr . 12 . 1664 .

John Brooks married Suſanna Hanmore . may . 25 . 1652 .
his ſonn John was Borne . march . 16 . 1660 . dead[2] .
his ſonn ſamuell was Borne . ſeptm^{r} . 6 . 62 .
his Daughtr elizabeth was Born . June . 27 . 64 .
his Daughter mary was Borne . march . 21 . 65 .
his Daughter Joanna was Borne . febury . 2 . 68 .
his Daughtr marcy was Borne . noum^{r} . 25 . 70 .

---

1 Written in black ink and crossed out.
2 Written in black ink.

his Daughter lidia was Borne . Aguſt . 7 . 1673 .
his dauter ſuſanna was Borne . ſeptem . 22 . 1675 .
his wife died . noum[r] . 7 . 76 .

[J]ohn Bancroft married Hanna Duper . Decm[r] . 3 . 1650 .
[his] ſonn John was Borne in Decmbr . 1651 .
[his ſonn] Nathanel was Borne . noum[r] . 19 . 1653 .
[his] ſonn [E]phraim was Borne . June . 15 . 1656 .
[hi]s Daugh[H]anna was Borne . aprel . 6 . 1659 .
[h]is Daughter ſara was Born . Decem[r] . 26 . 1661 .

[W]illiam Buell on dauter not ſet in plac .
his Daughtr Abigall . was Borne . febury . 12 . 1655 .

C . Aron capten Cook .
his Daughter Joanna was Borne or Baptiſed . aguſt . 5 . 1638 .
his sonn Aron was Baptiſed . febury . 21 . 1640 .
[his] Daughter mirriam Baptiſed . march . 12 . 1642 .
[his ſo]nn moſes was Baptiſed . noum[r] . 16 . 1645 .
[his ſ]onn ſamuell was Borne . noumb[r] . 21 . 1650 .
[his D]aughtr eliſabeth was Born . aguſt . 7 . 1653 .
[his] ſonn Noah . was Borns . June . 14 . 1657 .

[Pet]er Brown aftr . D .

[37] Daniell Clark married mary Newbery . June . 13 . 1644 .
his ſonn Joſias was Borne January . 21 . 1648 .
his Daughter eliſabeth was Borne . octo . 28 . 1651 .
his ſonn Danill was Borne . Aprell . 4 . 1654 .
his ſonn John was Borne . Aprell . 10 . 1656 .

his Daughter mary was Born . ſeptmr . 22 . 1658 .
his ſonn ſamuell was Borne . July . 6 . 1661 .
his Daughter ſary was Borne . aguſt . 7 . 1663 .
his Daughter Hanna was Borne . aguſt . 29 . 1665 . Dead .
his ſonn Nathanell waſs Borne . ſeptmr . 8 . 1666 .

Nathanell cook married . lidea vore . Juen . 29 . 1649
his Daughtr Sara was Borne . Juen . 28 . 1650 .
his Daughter lidia was Born . Janury . 9 . 1652 .
his Daughter Hanna was Borne . ſeptmr . 21 . 55 .
his ſonn Nathanell was Born . may . 13 . 1658 .
his Daughtr Abigall was Born . march . 1 . 1659 .
his ſonn John was Borne . Aguſt . 3 . 1662 .
his ſonn Joſia was Born . Decmr . 22 . 1664 .

John Caſs .
his Daughter mary was Borne . June 22 . 1660 .
his ſonn John was Borne . noumbr . 5 . 1662 .
his ſonn William was Born . June . 5 . 1665 .
his ſonn ſamucll was Borne . June . 1 . 1667 .
his ſonn Richard was Borne . Aguſt . 27 . 69 .
[Sa]ra caff borne Aprell . 14 . 1676 .

[38] D . Thomas Dewey marred francſ clark . march . 22 . 38 .
his ſonn Thomas was Born . febury . 16 . 1639 .
his ſonn Joſia was Baptiſed . ocobr . 10 . 1641 .
his Daughtr Anna was Baptiſed . octo . 15 . 1643 .
his ſonn Iſrell was Borne . ſeptmr . 25 . 1645 . Ded[1]
his ſonn Jededia was Borne . deſemr . 15 . 1647 .
thire father Dyed . Aprell . 27 . 1648 .

1 Written in black ink.

Thomas Deble .
his ſonn Iſrell was Borne . Aguſt . 29 . 1637 .
his ſonn Ebenezr was Baptiſed . ſeptm^r^ . 26 . 41 . Dead[1]
his Daughtr Hepſiba was Baptiſed . Decm^r^ . 25 . 42 .
his ſonn Samuell was Baptiſed . march . 24 . 43 .
born 19 feburi
his Daughter miriam was Baptiſed . Decem^r^ . 7 . 45 .
his ſonn Thomas was Borne . ſeptm^r^ . 3 . 1647 .
his wif dyed may . 14 . 1681 .

[Isrell] Deble married eliſabeth Hull . noum^r^ . 28 . 1661 .
his ſonn Joſias was Borne . may . 15 . 1667 .
his ſonn Thomas was Borne . ſeptm^r^ . 16 . 1670 .
his Daughtr eliſabeth was Borne . march . 27 . 1673 .
his ſonn georg[2] was Born Janury . 25 . 75 .
his ſonn John was born aguſt ye 18 . 78 . bapiſd . 6 . octobr . ded

Ebenezer Deble maried mary wakefilld . octo . 27 . 63 .
his Daughter mary was Borne Decem^r^ . 24 . 1664 .
his ſonn wakefild was Borne . ſepm^r^ . 15 . 1667 .
his Daughtr martha was Borne . marc . 10 . 1669 . dead
his ſonn John was Borne . febury . 9 . 1673 .
his ſonn ebeneſer was Borne . Aguſt . 18 . 1671 .

[39] Samuell Deble married Hepſiba Bartlet . Janury . 21 . 6[8]
his Daughtr Abigayl he had by his formr wife . Janury . 19 . 66 .
his Daughtr Hepſiba . by this wif . borne . Decm^r^ . 19 . 1669 .
his Daughter Joanna . was Borne . otobr . 24 . 1672 .

---

1 Written in black ink.
2 First written John

ſamuell his ſonn waſ borne Aprell . 13 . 1675 . Dyed ffeb . 8 . 75
his 2 ſamuell borne may ye 4 . 1677 .
minwell his dafter born febuary . 17 . 1680 .

Job Drake married mary wolcot . Juen . 25 . 1646 .
his Daughtr Abigayl was Borne . ſeptm^{r} . 28 . 1648 .
his Daughter mary was Borne . Deſem^{r} . 12 . 1649 .
his ſonn Jobe was Borne . march . 28 . 1652 .
his Daughter eliſabeth was Born . noum . 14 . 1654 .
his ſonn Joſeph was Borne . Aprell . 16 . 1657 . dead
his Daughtr Hepſiba was Borne . July . 14 . 1659 .
his Daughter Heſter was Borne . octobr . 10 . 1662 .

John Drake married Hanna moore . no[ ]
his ſonn John was Borne . ſeptem^{r} . 14 . 1649 .
his ſonn Job was Borne . Juen . 15 . 1651 .
his Daughtr Hanna was Borne . aguſt . 8 . 1653 .
his ſonn enock was Borne . Deſembr . 8 . 1655 .
his Daughtr Ruth was Borne . deſem^{r} . 1 . 1657 .
his ſonn Simon was Borne . octo . 28 . 1659 .
his Daughter Lidia was Borne . Janury . 26 . 1661 .
his Daughtr mary . was Borne . Janury . 29 . 1666 .
his Dautr eliſabeth was Borne . July . 22 . 1664 .
his Daughtr mindwell born noumbr . 10 . 1671 .
his ſon Joſeph was borne Juen . 26 . 74 . baptiſed ye . 28 day
[(Job)] Drak mared eliſabeth Aluard . marc . 20 . 1671 .
[h]is ſonn Jonathan was Borne . Janury . 4 . 1672 .
[h]is daughter Eliſabeth was born . noum^{r} . 2 . 1675

[40] Henery Denſlo .
his Daughter ſuſana was Borne . ſeptm^{r} . 3 . 1646 .

his Daughtr mary was Borne . Aprel . 10 . 1651 .
his Daughtr Ruth was Borne . feptem^{r} . 19 . 1653 .
his Daughtr Abigayl was Borne . febury . 6 . 1655 .
his Daughtr Debora was Borne . Decmbr . 21 . 1657 . maried[1]
his fonn Samuell was Borne . Decmbr . 19 . 1659 .
his Daughter Hanna was Borne . march . 1 . 1661 .
his Daughtr elifabet was Borne . febury . 11 . 1665 .

John Denflow married mary egelfton . Juen . 7 . 1655 .
[ ] fonn John waf Borne . Aguft . 13 . 1656 .
[ ] Daughter mary was Born . march . 10 . 1658 .
[ ] fonn Thomas was Borne . Aprell . 22 . 1661 .
[ ]Daughtr rebeca was . Borne . may . 29 . 1663 .
his fonn Jofeph was Borne . Aguft . 12 . 1665 .
his fonn Beniamen was Born . march . 30 . 1668 .
his fonn Abraham was Borne . marc . 8 . 1669 .
his fonn georg was Borne . Aprell . 8 . 1672 .
his fonn Ifack was Borne . Aprell . 12 . 1674 .
his daughtr Abigall was born noumbr . 7 . 1677 .
July . 14 . 78 . baptifed .

Jacob Drake married mary Bifell . Aprell . 12 . 1649 .
now 74 . it is . 25 yer . and neuer had child .
his mothor that lived with him a wido m[ ]ny y[ ]
hir hir hufband Jacobs father . dyed . aguft . 18 . [ ]
and now octobr . 7 . 1681 . Jacobs mother dy[ ]
hir 100 yer of age . haue liued a wido . 22 . y[ ]

[41] Peter Brown married mary Gillet . July . 15 . 1658 .

1 This word is written in black ink.

his Daughtr mary was Borne . may . 2 . 1659 .
his Daughtr Hanna was Borne . ſeptm . 29 . 1660 .
his Daughtr Abigayl was Borne . Aguſt . 8 . 1662 .
his Daughtr Hepſiba was Borne . noum^r . 19 . 1664 .
his ſonn Peter was Borne . march . 2 . 1666 .
his ſonn John[1] was Borne . Janury . 8 . 1668 .
his ſonn cornelus was Borne . July . 30 . 1672 .
his Daughtr Heſter was Borne . may . 22 . 1673 .
his ſonn Jonathan, omited in his pro
per plac, was born . march . 30 . 1670 .
Ezabell his daughter born Juen . 9 . 76 .
debora his daftr born . febury 12 nit be for . 1678 .
Sara his daftr born aguſt . 20 . 81 .

Edward Chapman married eliſabeth fox in Ingland
his ſonn Henery born here . July . 4 . 1663 .
his Daughtr mary Borne . aguſt . 23 . 1664 . Dead
his Daughtr mary was Born . octo . 27 . 1665 .
his Daughtr eliſabeth Born . Janury . 15 . 1667 .
his ſonn ſimon was Born . aprel . 30 . 1669 .
his Daughtr Hanna Borne . may . 3 . 1671 .
his Daughtr margret Born . march . 7 . 1672 :
his Daughter ſara Born . may . 24 . 75 .

Henery Curtic married eliſabeth Abel . may . 13 . 1645 .
his ſonn ſamuell curtic was Born . Aprell . 26 . 1649 .
his ſonn Nathanel curtic was Borne . July . 15 . 1651 .

ſamuell croſs maried ye wido chapman . July . 12 . 1677 .

1 cornelus crossed out.

Juen . 11 . 78 . a daftr born . Hanna crofs .
decmbr . 10 . 79 . his fonn famuell borne . and dyed that day
his daftr Hana died July . 7 . 1680 .

[42] E James enno and Anna Bedwell ware maryed . Aguft . 18 . 1648 .
his Daughter Sara was Borne . Juen . 15 . 1649 .
his fonn James enno was Borne . octobr . 30 . 1651 .
his fonn John enno was Borne . Decembr . 2 . 1654 .
his wife dyed octor . 7 . 79 . buried ye 8 day

Thomas egelfton fonn of Begat egelfton . Borne . Aguft . 26 . 1638 .
marcy egelfton was Borne . may . 29 . 1641 .
Sara egelfton was Borne . march . 28 . 1643 .
Rebeca egelfton was Borne . Decmr . 8 . 1644 .
Abigayl egelfton was Borne . Juen . 12 . 1648 .
Jofeph egelfton was Baptifed . march . 30 . 1651 .
Beniamen egelfton was Borne Decemr . 18 . 1653 .
Begat egelfton Dyed feptemr . 1 . 74 . nere 100 yer ould.

Jofia elefworth and elizabeth Holcom . ware maried . noumr . 16 . 1654
[his] fonn Jofias elefworth was Born . Noumr . 5 . 1655 .
[El]izabeth his Daughter was Borne . Noumr . 11 . 1657 .
[ ]y elefworth was Borne . may . 7 . 1660 .
[ ] elefworth was Borne . Decemr . 7 . 1662 .
Thom[a]s elefworth was Borne . feptmr . 2 . 1665 .
Jonathan elefworth was Borne . Juen . 28 . 1669 .
John elefworth was Borne . october . 7 . 1671 .
Job fonn of Jofias elefwort was born . Aprel . 13 . 167[ ]
[ ]ptifd [ ]to . 10 . 75 .
Beniamen his fonn was borne . January . 19 . 1676 .

James ſon of James egeſton was borne . Janery . 1 . 1656 . Dead
his ſon John egelſton was borne . march . 27 . 1659 .
his ſonn Thomas egelſton was born . July . 27 . 1661 .
his Daughter Heſter egelſton was borne . decmr . 1 . 166[ ]
his ſonn Nathanell was Borne . Auguſt . 15 . 1666 .
his ſonn Iſack egelſton was Born . febury . 27 . 1668 .
his Daughter Abigall was Born ſeptmr . 1 . 1671 .
his Daughter Debroa was Born . may . 1 . 1674
his Daughter Hanna was Born deſembr[2] . 19 . 1676 .

[43] ff John ſonn of walter ffylar was Borne . ſeptmr . 12 . 1642 .
Zurobabel fylar was Borne Decembr . 23 . 1644 .

Zurobabel fylar and Experenc Strong ware maried . may . 27 . 1669 .
his ſonn Thomas fylar was borne . January . 25 . 1669 .
his Daughter Jane fylar was borne . January . 1 . 1671 .
his ſonn Zurobabel was borne . octobr . 31 . 1673 . Dead
his . 2 . ſonn Zurobell was borne . decembr . 25 . 1674 .
his ſonn John fillar borne march . ye 2 . baptiſed ye . 11 . 16[ ]

John ffylar and eliſabeth Dolman ware married . octobr . 17 . 1672

ff William filly and margret his wif ware married . ſeptemr . 2 . 164[ ]
his ſonn ſamuell filly was borne . ſeptember . 24 . 1643 .
his ſonn John filly was Borne . December . 15 . 1645 .
his Daughter mary filly . was Born .
his Daughter eliſabeth filly was Borne . march . 4 . 1650 .
[ ]Daughter Abigal filly was Borne . Auguſt . 21 . 1658
his Daughter Debroa filly was Borne . march . 21 . 1661 .

2 Jauury crossed out.

his ſonn William filly was Borne . march . 7 . $16\frac{64}{65}$.

[44] Samuell ffilly married Anna gillet . october . 29 . 1663 .
his Daughter Anna filly was Borne . Aguſt . 16 . 1664 .
his Daughter mary filly was Borne . Aprell . 12 . 1667 . dyed iun 168[ ][1]
his Daughter Abigayl felly was Borne . Janury . 20 . 1668 . Dead
his ſonn ſamuell filly was Borne . Aprel . 2 . 1670 . dead
his ſonn Jonathan ffilly was Borne . noumbr . 30 . 1672 .
his ſonn ſamuell ffilly was Borne . march . 7 . 1673 . kiled wth a cart[2]
his ſonn Joſia ffilly was Born Janury . 21 . 1675
his ſonn John was born . febry . 10 . baptiſed . 17 . 1677 .
Abigayl daftr of ſamuell filly . born Jan^r^ . 3 . 1679 .

Ambrous fowller married Joone Aluard . may . 6 . 1646 .
his Daughtr Abigayl fowler was Borne . march 1 . 1646 .
his ſonn John fowler was Borne . noumbr . 19 . 1648 .
his Daughter mary was Borne . may . 15 . 1650 .
his ſonn ſamuell fouler Borne . noumber 18 . 1652 .
his Daughter Hanna fowler was Borne . deſcembr . 20 . 1654 .
[his] Daughter eliſabeth fowler was Borne . deſembr . 2 . 1656 .
[his] ſonn Ambrous fowler was Borne . may . 8 . 1658 .

[ ] of ſamuell forward was Borne . July . 23 . 1671 .
[ ] of ſamuell forward was Borne . noumb . 10 . 1674 .

[Samuel] Grant was Borne . nouember ye 12 . 1631 . in Dorcheſtr .
He was married to mary Porter . may . 27 . 1658 .
his ſonn ſamuell grant was Borne . Aprell . 20 . 1659 .
his ſonn John grant was Borne . Aprell . 24 . 1664 .

1 This date may be 1683.
2 Written in black ink.

his ſonn mathew grant was Borne . ſeptmr . 22 . 1666 .
his ſonn Joſia grant was Borne . march . 19 . 1668 .
his ſonn Nathanell grant was Borne . Aprel . 14 . 1672 .
his Daughter mary was borne Janury . 23 . 75 .
his Daftr ſara was borne January . 19 . 1678 . deyed
baptiſed febry . 2 . 78

ſamuel grant was maried to anna fillie
deſember 6 1683 .
his daughter anna was born ſeptember 2 1684

[45] Tahan Grant was Borne febury . 3 . 1633 . in Dorcheſter
He was married to Hanna Palmer . January . 22 . 1662 .
his ſonn mathew grant was Borne . January . 4 . 1663 . Dead
his ſonn Tahan grant was Borne . ſeptemr . 27 . 1665 .
his Daughter hanna was Borne . Juen . 8 . 1668 .
his ſonn Thomas grant was Borne . febury . 20 . 1670 .
his Joſeph grant his ſonn was Borne . may . 14 . 1673 .
his Daughter ſara was Born ſeptmr 19 baptiſd that day . 1675 .
his Dafter mary was Born ocobr 23 . 78 . baptiſed noumr . 3 day
another ſonn was born dead nouembr 11 . 1680 .

John Grant was Borne . Aprell . 30 . 1642 . in windſor .
He was married to mary Hull . Aguſt . 2 . 1666 .
his ſonn John Grant was Borne . octobr . 20 . 167[ ]
his Daughter mary was Borne . Aprell . 26 . 16[ ]
his Daughter eliſſabeth was Born . July . 10 . 77 . baptiſed [
his dafter Abigal as born . Janury . 27 . 1679 .
ſhee was baptiſed by mr foſter at Hartford July 17 . 168[ ]

Jonathan Gillet sen[r] .
his Daughter anna was his firſt bor̄ in windſor . Decem[r] . 29 . 1639 .
his ſonn Joſeph gillet was Baptiſed . July . 25 . 1641 .
his ſonn ſamuell gillet was Baptiſed . Janury . 22 . 1642 .
his ſonn John gillet was Borne . octobr 5 . 1644 .
his Daughter Abbigayel was Baptiſed . Juen . 28 . 1646 .
his ſonn Jeremia gillet was Borne . febury . 12 . 1647 .
his ſonn Joſias gillet was Baptiſed . July . 14 . 1650 .

Jonathan gillet iun[r] married mary kelſey . Aprell . 23 . 1661 .
his Daughter mary gillet was Borne . octobr . 21 . 1667 .
his ſonn Jonathan gillet was Born . febury . 18 . 1670 .
his ſonn william gillet was Borne Decem[r] . 4 . 1673 .
his wife dyed . Aprell . 18 . 76 . he married meriam
Deble decmbr . 14 . 76 . hir ſonn Thomas was borne . may . 31 . 1678
dyed Ju[ ] 11
his ſonn ebenezr was born . octobr . 28 . 1679 . dyed [?] 19 . 7 [ ]
[?] ſon born decmbr 17 . 80 . ſamuell

cornelis gillet married .
his Daughter Priſſella was Borne . January . 23 . 1659 . Dead
his . 2 . Daughter Priſſilla was Borne . march . 30 . 1661 .
his Daughter Abigail was Borne . ſeptm[r] . 20 . 1663 .
his ſonn cornelius Gillet was Borne . Decm[r] . 15 . 1665 .
his Daughter marey gillet was Borne . aguſt . 12 . 1668 .
his Daughter Heſter gillet was Borne . may . 24 . 1671 .
his Daughter ſarah gillet was Borne . January . 3 . 1673 .
his Daughter Joanna gillet was Borne . Aprell
ye 22 . 1676 . baptiſed ye 23 day . 1676 .
his ſonn was borne Juen . 10 . 1671 . his ſonn nathanell was

borne ye 4 of may . 1673 . Hanna was borne 30 ianury . 1674 .[1]
daniel gillite was borne Juen : 30 1678[2]

Joſeph gillet married
his ſonn Joſep was Borne . noumber . 2 . 1664 .
his Daughter eliſabet was Borne . Juen ye . 12 . 1666 .
his Daughter mary was Borne . ſeptemr . 10 . 1667 .
[his ſon]n Jonathan gillet was Borne . Aguſt . 11 . 1669 . baptiſed[3]
[ ] 77[3] . thes entred after Thomas Dewey .

[Gille]t married marcy Barber . July . 8 . 1669 .
[his ſonn] John Gillet was Borne . Aguſt . 6 . 1673 .
[his ſonn] Thomas gillet was Born July . 18 . Baptiſed 23 . 1676 .
his ſonn ſamuell gillet was Borne febur . ye 16 . 1677 .
his ſonn nathanell was brn octobr . 3 . 1680
baptiſed at hartford october . 30 . 1681

Nathan Gillet married
his Daughter eliſabeth was Borne . octobr . 6 . 1639 .
his Daughter Abia was Born . Aguſt . 22 . 1641 .
his Daughter Rebeca was Borne . Juen . 14 . 1646 .
his ſonn elias gillet was Borne . July . 1 . 1649 .
his Daughter ſarah was Borne . July . 13 . 1651 .
his ſonn Beniamen was Borne . Aguſt . 29 . 1653 . Dead
his ſonn Nathan Gillet was Borne . Aguſt . 17 . 1655 .
his Daughter Rebeca was Borne . Decmr . 8 . 1657 .

---

1 This and the preceding line are crossed out.
2 Not in Matthew Grants handwriting.
3 This word and date are crossed out.

[47] Thomas gunn .
his Daughter eliſabeth was Borne . octobr . 14 . 1640 . dead
his Daughter Debroa was Borne . febury . 21 . 1641 .
his Daughter mehetabell was Borne . July . 28 . 1644 .
his ſonn . John gunn was Borne . July . 8 . 1647 .

Edward Griſwold
his Daughter Ann was . Baptiſed . Juen . 19 . 1642 .
his Daughter mary was Baptiſed . octobr . 13 . 1644 .
his Daughter Debroa was Baptiſed . Juen . 28 . 1646 .
his ſonn Joſeph griſwold was Baptiſed . march . 12 . 1647 .
his ſonn ſamuell griſwold was Baptiſed . nom^{r} . 18 . 1649 . dead
his ſonn John griſwold was Baptiſed . Aguſt . 1 . 1652 .

---

georg Griſwold married mary Holcom . octobr . 3 . [ ]
his ſonn Daniell griſwold was Borne . octobr . 1 . 1656
his ſonn Thomas griſwold was Borne . ſeptem^{r} . 29 . 165[ ]
his ſonn edward griſwold was Borne . march . 19 . 16$\frac{60}{61}$.
his Daughter mary was Borne . ſeptembr . 28 . 1663 .
his ſonn Georg Griſwold was Born . Decem^{r} . 3 . 1665 .
his ſonn John Griſwold was Borne . ſeptm^{r} . 17 . 1668 .
his ſonn Beniamen griſwald was Borne . Aprel . 16 . 1671 .
his Daughter Debrow was Borne . may . 30 . 1674 .
his Daughter Abigayl was Born . octob^{r} . 31 . 1676 .

Joſeph Griſwold married mary Gaylars . July . 14 . 1670 .
his Daughter mary was Borne . march . 16 . 1670 .
his ſonn Joſep griſwold was Borne Janury . 24 . 1677 .

[48] William Gaylar iun^{r} married Ann Porter . febuary . 24 . 1641 .
his Daughter Ann . was Borne . Aprell . 24 . 1645 .

his Daughter Hanna was Borne . Janury . 30 . 1646 .
his fonn John gaylard was Borne . Janury . 27 . 1648 .
his fonn william Gaylar was Borne . febury . 25 . 1650 .
his fonn Hezeciah gaylar was Born . febury . 11 . 1652 . Ded[1]
his fonn Jofia gaylard was Borne . febury . 13 . 1654 .
his fonn Nathanell gaylar was Borne . feptmr . 3 . 1656 .
william gaylar ye father of thes children dyed . Decmr . 14 . 1656 .

Walter Gaylar marryed . mary ftebens . aprell . 1648 .
his fonn Jofeph gaylar was Borne . may . 13 . 1649 .
his Daughter mary was Born . march . 19 . 1650 .
[his] Daughter Joanna was Borne . febury . 5 . 1652 .
his fonn Beniamen Gaylar was born . Aprell . 12 . 1655 .
his fonn Ifack was Borne . Juen . 21 . 1657 . dead .
his wife Dyed . Juen . 29 . 1657 .
[ ] he marryed a fecond wife farah Rockwell . marc . 22 . 1659
his fonn eliazer gaylar was Borne . march . 7 . 1662 .
his Daughter fara was Borne . Aprell . 13 . 1665 .

Jofep fonn of walter gaylar . married farah ftandly . July . 14 . 1670 .
his Daughter fara was Borne . July . 11 . 1671 .
his fonn Jofhep gaylar was Born . Aguft . 22 . 1673 .
his fonn John gaylar was born Aguft . 21 . 77 . baptifed may . 12 . 78 . windfr

Jofia gillet & Johana Tainter ware maried by mr John Allyn . Juen . 30 . 1676 . his fon Jofia was born . noumbr 24 . 1678 . baptifed ye 1 of decembr . 78 .

[49] Samuell Gaylar married Elifabeth Hull . Defemr . 4 . 1646
his Daughter elifabeth was Borne . octobr . 4 . 1647 .

---

1 This word is written in blue ink.

his Daughter mary was Borne . noumbr . 10 . 1649 .
his Daughter ſara was Borne . Janury . 18 . 1651 .
his Daughter Abigayl was Borne . ſeptm[r] . 29 . 1653 .
his ſonn ſamuell gaylar was Born . July . 1657 .
his Daughter martha was Borne . Juen . 1660 .

John Gaylar married mary Drak . noumbr . 17 . 1653 .
his ſonn John Gaylar was Borne . Juen . 15 . 1656 . Dead .
his Daughter mary was Borne . Janury . 19 . 1663 .
his . 2 . ſonn John gaylar was Born . Juen . 23 . 1667 .
his Daughter eliſabeth was Born . febury . 19 . 1670 .

John Griffen married Anna Bancroft . may . 13 . 164[7]
his Daughter Hanna was Borne . July . 4 . 1649 .
his Daughter mary was Borne . march . 1 . 1651 .
his Daughter ſara was Borne . Decem[r] . 25 . 1654 .
his ſonn John grifen was Borne . octobr . 20 . 1656 .
his ſonn Thomas Grifen was Born . octobr . 3 . 1658 .
his Daughter Abigaill was Born . noum[r] . 12 . 1660 .
his Daughter mindwel was Born . febry . 11 . 1662 .
his Daughter Ruth was Borne . Janury . 21 . 1665 .
his ſonn Epharam grifen was Borne . march . 1 . 1668 .
his ſonn nathanell griffen was born may . 31 . 1673 .

Jacob Gibbes married eliſabeth Androus . Decm[r] . 4 . 1657 .
his Daughter mary was Borne . Aprell . 21 . 1659 .
his Daughter Abigayl was Born . Janury . 7 . 1661 .
his ſonn Jacob gibbs was Borne . Decem[r] . 1 . 1664 . Dead
his . 2 . ſonn Jacob gibbes was Borne . Juen . 22 . 1666 .
his Daughter ſara was Borne . febury . 28 . 1668 .
his Daughter eliſabeth was Born . aprel . 1 . 1672 .

his Daughter [ ] born ſeptemr . 13 . 16 [ ]

[50] Samuell Gibbes married Hepſiba Deble . aprell . 15 . 1664 .
his Daughter Hepſiba was Borne Janury . 12 . 1664 .
his Daughter Patienc was Borne . Dcemr . 2 . 1666 .
his Daughter elizabeth was Borne . Janury . 30 . 1668 .
his Daughter Joanna was Borne . march . 26 . 1671 .
his Daughter experenc was Borne . Aprell . 4 . 1673 .
his Daughter cattarn was Born Aprell . 29 . 1675 . Ded .
his ſonn ſamuell was Born Aprell ye 16 . 1677 .
his ſonn Jonathan was borne febry . ye 16 . 1679

H Thomas Holcom .
his Daughter Abigayl Born or Baptiſed . Janury . 6 . 38 .
his ſonn Joſua Holcom . Baptiſed . ſeptemr . 27 . 1640 .
his Daughter ſara . Borne . Aguſt . 14 . 1642 . Dead
his ſonn Benaga Holcom . was Born . Juen . 23 . 1644 .
his Daughter Debroa was Borne . octobr . 15 . 1646 . Dead
his ſonn Nathanell Holcom . Borne . noumbr . 4 . 1648 .
his . 2 . Daughter Debroa Borne februry . 15 . 1650 .
his ſonn Jonathan was Borne . march . 23 . 1652 . Dead[1]

Joſua Holcom married Ruth ſharwod . Juen . 4 . 1663 .
his Daughter Ruth . was Borne . may . 26 . 1664 .
his ſonn Thomas Holcom was Borne . march . 30 . 1666 .
his Daughter ſara was Borne . Juen . 23 . 1668 .

Benaga Holcom married ſara eunos . Aprell . 11 . 1667 .
his ſonn Benaga Holcom was Borne . Aprell . 16 . 1668 .
his ſonn James Holcom was Borne . october . 13 . 1671 .

1 This word is written in black ink.

William Hayden .
his ſonn Daniell Hayden was Borne . ſeptem^{r} . 2 . 1640
his ſonn Nathanell Hayden was Borne . febury . 2 . 1643 .
his Daughter mary was Borne . Juen . 6 . 1648 .

[51] Danell Haydon married Hanna Wilcokſon . march . 17 . 1664
his ſonn Danell Haydon was Borne . october . 5 . 1666 .
his Daughter Hanna was Borne . nouembr . 9 . 1668 .
his ſonn Nathanell was Borne . march . 28 . 1671 . Dead
his ſonn William Hayden was Borne . Aprell . 27 . 1673 . Dead[1]
his 2 ſonn william was Borne January . 1 . 1675 .

John Hofford married Phillup Trall . nouem^{r} . 5 . 1657 .
his ſonn William Hofford was Born . octobr . 25 . 1658 .
his ſonn John Hofford was Borne . octobr . 16 . 1660 .
his ſonn Timothy Hofford was Borne . octobr . 20 . 1662 .
his Daughter Heſter was Borne . may . 27 . 1664 .
his Daughter ſara was Borne . ſeptem^{r} . 27 . [1666]
his ſonn ſamuell Hofford was Borne . Juen . [2 . 1669]
his ſonn Nathanell Hofford was Born . aguſt [. 19 . 167]
his Daughter mary was Borne . Aprell . 12 [. 1674]
obadia ſonn of John Hofford was born ſeptmb[ ] . 167[ ]

Nicolas Hayt married ſuſana Joyce . July . 12 . 1646 .
his ſonn ſamuell Hayt was Borne . may . 1 . 1647 .
his ſonn Jonathan Hayt was Borne . Juen . 7 . 1649 .
his ſonn Dauid Hayt was Borne . Aprel . 22 . 1651 .
his ſonn Daniell Hayt was Borne . Aprell . 10 . 1653 . Dead

1 This word is written in black ink.

Robard Hayward
his Daughter Taphath was Borne Janury . 1 . 1646 .
his Daughter Rebeca was Born Aguſt . 17 . 1648 .
his Daughter Hefter was Borne . Juen . 8 . 1651 . Dead
his Daughter lidea was Borne . Juen . 13 . 1655 . Dead[1]
his ſonn Ephram Hayward was Borne January . 11 . 1656 .

[52] John Hakes .
his ſonn Iſack Hakes was Borne . Aguſt . 11 . 1650 . Dead . in . 59 .
his Daughter mary . was Borne . may . 23 . 1652 .
his Daughter Johana was Borne . febury . 8 . 1653 . Dead
his ſonn eliezer Hakes was Borne . Decmbr . 20 . 1655 .
his Daughter ſara was Borne . ſeptemr . 29 . 1657 .
his ſonn Jerſom Hakes was Borne . Aprell . 12 . 1659 .
before all theſe ware borne .
his ſonn John Hakes was Borne . Aguſt . 13 . 1643 .
his ſonn Nathanell Hakes . was Borne . febury . 16 . 1644 .
his Daughter elizabeth was Borne . January . 10 . 1646 .
his Daughter Anna Haks was Borne . octobr . 1 . 1648 .

Joſias Hull married eliſabeth Loomys . may . 20 . 1641 .
his ſonn Joſias Hull was Borne ſeptembr . 1642 . Dead
[his ſonn] John Hull was Borne . Deſembr . 17 . 1644 .
[his Dau]ghter eliſabeth was Born . febury . 18 . 1646 .
[his Dau]ghter mary was Borne . octobr . 2 . 1648 .
[his Daug]hter martha was Borne . Juen . 10 . 1650 .
[his ſonn] Joſeph Hull was Borne . aguſt . 10 . 1652 .
his Daughter Sara was Borne . aguſt . 9 . 1654 .
his Daughter naomy was Borne . febury . 17 . 1656 .
his Daughter Rebeca was Borne . Aguſt . 10 . 1659 .

Capten Tamas

1 This word is written in black ink.

his fonn georg Hull was Borne . Aprel . 28 . 1662 . Dead[1]
his fonn Thomas Hull was Born . may . 29 . 1665 .
[ ] Jofias Hull dyed . noum^{r} . 16 . 75 .

---

micall Houmfery married Priffilla Grant . octobr . 14 . 1647 .
his fonn John Houmfery was borne . Juen . 7 . 1650 .
his Daughter mary was Borne . octobr . 24 . 1653 .
his fonn famuell Humfery was Borne . may . 15 . 1656 .
his Daughter martha was Borne . octobr . 5 . 1663 .
his Daughter fara was Borne . march 6 . 1658 .
his Daughter Abigayl was Borne . march . 23 . 1665 .
his Daughter Hanna was Borne . october . 21 . 1669 .

[53] Luke Hill married mary Hout . may . 6 . 1651 .
his Daughter liddya was Borne . febury . 18 . 1651 .
his Daughter mary[2] was Borne . feptem^{r} . 20 . 1654 .
his fonn Tahan Hill was Borne . noumbr . 23 . 1659 .
his fonn Luke Hill was Borne . march . 6 . 1661 .
his Daughte Abigayl was Borne . Aprell . 16 . 1664 .
his Daughter elifabeth was Born . octobr . 8 . 1666 .
his fonn John Hill was borne . noumber . 28 . 1668 .

Anthony Howkins .
his Daughter mary was Borne . July . 16 . 1644 .
his Daughter Ruth was Borne . octobr . 24 . 1649 .
his fonn John Howkins was Born . febury . 18 . 1651 .

---

1 This word is written in black ink.
2 Hanna first written and crossed out.

Georg Jeffery .
his Daughter mary was Borne . Juen . 1 . 1669
his daughter Hanna . was born . Aguſt . 23 . 1671 .
his daughter elizabeth was born . decmbr . 24 . 1675

L John Loomys marryed Eliſabeth fcot . febua[ry 3 . 1648 .]
his fonn John loomys was Borne . noumber . 9 . 1649 .
his fonn Joſeph loomys was Borne noumbr . 7 . 1651 .
his fonn Thomas loomys was Born . deſembr . 3 . 1653 .
his fonn ſamuell loomys was Borne . Juen . 29 . 1655 . Dead
his fonn Daniell loomys was Borne . Juen . 16 . 1657 .
his fonn James Loomys was Borne . ſeptm^{r} . 19 . 1659 . Dead in . 69 .
his fonn Timothy loomys was Borne . July . 27 . 1661 .
his fonn Nathanell loomys was Borne . July . 8 . 1663 .
his fonn Daued loomys was Borne . may . 30 . 1665 . Dead in Juen . 65
his . 2 . fonn ſamuell loomys was Borne . Aguſt . 12 . 1666 .
his fonn Iſack loomys was Borne . Aguſt . 31 . 1668 .
his Daughter eliſabeth was Borne . may . 8 . 1671 .
his Daughter mary was Borne . Aguſt . 7 . 1673 . Dead may . 14 . 7[ ][1]

[54] Joſeph Loomys marryed Sara Hill . ſeptem^{r} . 17 . 1646 .
his Daughter ſara was Borne . July . 22 . 1647 . Dead in . 54 .
his fonn Joſeph loomys was Born . July . 15 . 1649 .
his fonn John Loomys . was Borne . octob^{r} . 1 . 1651 .
his Daughter mary was Borne . Aguſt . 3 . 1653 .
his . 2 . Daughter ſara was Borne . Aprel . 1 . 1660 . Dyed
his Daughter Hanna was Borne . febury . 2 . 1661 .
his fonn mathew loomys was Born . noum^{r} . 4 . 1664 .
his fonn Nathanell Loomys was Born . Aguſt . 8 . 1673 .

1 The entry of death is in black ink.

his ſonn ſtephen was born ſeptm^{r} ye 1 . 1668 .
his ſonn James was born october 31 . 1669 .
his ſonn Iſack born . october . 28 . 1677 .
Joſep lomis mared mary ſharwod Juen 28 . 1659[1] .

Thomas Loomys married Hanna fox . noumber . 1 . 1653 .
his ſonn Thomas loomys was Borne . octobr . 29 . 1654 . Dyed .
his . 2 . ſonn Thomas Loomye was Borne . march . 17 . 1655 .
his Daughter Hanna was Borne . febury . 8 . 1657 .
his Daughter mary was Borne . Janury . 16 . 1659 .
[ ] wifie Hanna dyed . Aprell . 25 . 1662 .
Thomas loomys maried his . 2 . wif mary Judg . Janury . 1 . 1662 .
his Daughter eliſabeth was Borne . Janury . 21 . 1663 .
his Daughtr ruth . was Borne . october . 16 . 1665 .
his Daughter ſara was Borne . febury . 1 . 1667 .
his ſonn Jeremya loomys was Born . July . 3 . 1670 . dyed
his Daughter maybell was Borne . october . 27 . 1672 .
his Daughter mindwell was Borne Aguſt . 6 . 1676 .
Baptiſed ye 13 day of aguſt . 76 .
his ſonn Beniamen . born . may . 20 . 79 . baptiſed . Juen . 1 . 79 .

[55] Nathanell Loomys married eliſabeth moore . noumber . 27 . [1653]
his Daughter eliſabeth was Borne . Aguſt . 7 . 1655 . maried[2] .
his ſonn Nathanell loomys was Borne . march . 20 . 16$\frac{5\ 6}{5\ 7}$.
his Daughter Abigayl was Borne . march . 27 . 1659 .
his ſonn Joſia loomys was Borne . febury . 17 . 1660 .
his ſonn Jonathan loomys was Born . march . 30 . 1664 .
his ſonn Dauid Loomys was Borne . Janury . 11 . 1667 .
his ſonn Hezekia loomys was Born . febury . 21 . 1668 .

1 This entry is written in the margin, perhaps at a later date.
2 This word is written in black ink.

his fonn mofes Loomys was Born . may . 15 . 1671 .
his Daughter mindwell was Born . July . 20 . 1673 . Dyed[1]
his fonn ebenefer loomys Born . march . 22 . 16$\frac{74}{75}$
his dafter mary lomis borne January ye 5 . 79 .
his daughter rebeck was born defembr 10 1682[2]

Samuell Loomy .
his Daughter Ruth was Borne . Juen . 14 . 1660 .
his Daughter fara was Borne . febury . 3 . 1662 .
his Daughter Joanna was Borne . octobr . 22 . 1665 .
his fonn Beniamen was Borne . febury . 11 . 166[7]
his fonn Nehemia loomys was Borne . July . 15 . 1670 .

m^{r} Nathanell chancy techer of ye church of chrift at windfo[r]
maried Abigayl Daughter of elder John ftrong . at norham[ ]
his fonne Ifack chancy was Borne . noumbr . 12 . 1673 .
feptembr ye 6 . 74 . ye night before and baptifed that day .
Kathren Daughter of m^{r} Nathanell Chancy was born Jan . 12 . 16[75]
and Baptifed ye 16 day .
his daughter Abigayl was born october ye 14 . 16[ ] that
day at night baptifed . born a . 11 . ye clock ye [ ] befor
his fonn charles was borne feptem^{r} . 3 . 79 . baptifed ye . 7 . day .
he died octo^{r} . 31 . 79 .

[56] Abigaile febru 14 1639
M . Decon John moore his children Born in windfor . ∧
are, his Daughter mindwell . was Borne . July . 10 . 1643
his fonn John moore was Borne . Decem^{r} . 5 . 1645
Decon moore dyed feptm^{r} . 18 . 77 . buried ye 19 . day .

1 This word is crossed out.
2 This entry is not in Matthew Grant's handwriting.

John moore married Hanna Goſe . ſeptemb . 21 . 1664 .
his ſonn John moore was Borne . Juen . 26 . 1665 .
his ſonn Thomas moore was Born . July . 25 . 1667 .
his ſonn ſamuell moore was Born . decem^r . 24 . 1669 .
his ſonn Nathanel moor was Borne . ſeptm^r . 20 . 1672 .
his ſonn edward moore was Borne march 2 . 1674 .
July . 5 . 79 . his ſonns Joſias and Joſep was borne

Samuell marſhall maried mary Wilton . may . 6 . 1652 .
his ſonn ſamuell marſhall was Borne . may . 27 . 1653 .
his Daughter lidia was Borne . febury . 18 . 1655 .
his [ſonn] Thomas marſhall was Born . Aprel . 23 . 1659 . Dead
his ſonn Dauid marſhall was Borne . July . 24 . 1661 .
his 2 . ſonn Thomas marſhall was Born . febury . 18 . 1663 .
his Daughter mary was Borne . may . 8 . 1667 .
his ſonn eliacem marſhall was Born . July . 10 . 1669 .
his ſonn John marſhall was Borne . Aprel . 10 . 1672 .
his Daughter elizabeth was borne . ſeptm^r . 27 . 1674 .

John mawdſly married mary Newbery . Deſem^r . 14 . 1664 .
his ſonn Beniamen mawdeſly was Borne . octobr . 13 . 1666 .
his Daughter margret was Borne . febury . 4 . 1668 .
his ſonn Joſeph mawdſly was Borne . Deſem^r . 21 . 1670 .
his Daughter mary was Borne . may . 1 . 1673 .
his ſonn conſider was borne noumer ye [?]
[?] 21 . 75 . [?]

[57] Timothy moſes was borne in febuary . 1670 .
martha moſes borne . march . 8 . 1672 .
John Moſes married mary Brown . may . 18 . 1653 .
his ſonn John moſes was Borne . Juen . 15 . 1654 .

his fonn william mofes was Born . feptm^{r} . 1 . 1656 . ded[1]
his fonn Thomas mofes was Born . Janury . 14 . 1658 . Dead July[1]
his Daughter mary borne . may . 13 . 1661 .
his Daughter fary born . febury . 2 . 1663 .
his Daughter margret born . Decmbr . 2 . 1663 .
his Daughter mindwell born Decmbr 13 . 1676

edward mefenger
his Daughter Darkes was Borne feptem^{r} . 23 . 1650 .
his fonn nathanell mefengr . Borne . Juen . 18 . 16[53]
his Daughter Deliuerenc . was Born . Aprel [7] 16[55]

Andrew moore married fara Phelps . febuary [15 . 1671]
his Daughter fara was Borne . Defembr . 6 . [ ]
his fonn Andrew moor . was borne febury . 15 . 1674 .
his daughtr Debora was born . may . 31 . 1677 .
his fonn Jonathan was borne febuary ye 6 . 79 .

Thomas mafkell married Bethia Parfons . may . 10 . 1660 .
his Daughter Bethia was Borne . march . 6 . 1660 . Dead .
his fonn Thomas mafkl . was Born . march . 19 . 1661 . Dead .
his Daughter Abigayl was Borne . noum^{r} . 27 . 1663 .
his . 2 . fonn Thomas was Borne . Janury . 2 . 1664 .
his fonn John John mafkl Borne . noum^{r} . 19 . 1667 .
his Daughter Elifabeth was Born . octo^{r} . 19 . 1669 .

Simon milles married . mary Buell . febury . 23 . 1656 .
his fonn famuell was Borne . Aprel . 23 . 1661 . Dead
his fonn fimon was Borne . Janury . 21 . 1661 . Dead
his fonn fimon baptifed may . 11 . 1679 .

1 These deaths are entered in black ink.

[58] mary Daughter of ſimon mills was Borne . Deſem^{r} . 8 . 1662 .
Simon ſonn of ſimon mills was Born . may . 1 . 1667 .
John ſonn of ſimon milles was Borne . Juen . 23 . 1668 .
ſara Daughtr of ſimon mills was Borne . ſeptm^{r} . 16 . 1670 .

N . Beniamen Newbery married mary Allyn . Juen . 11 . 1646 .
his Daughter Mary was Borne . march . 10 . 1647 . maried[1]
his Daughter ſara was Borne . Juen . 14 . 1650 . maried[1]
his Daughter Hanna was Borne . Deſm^{r} . 22 . 1652 . Dead
his Daughter Rebeca was Borne . may . 2 . 1655 . maried[1]
his ſonn Thomas Newbery Born . ſeptm^{r} . 1 . 1657 .
his Daughter Abigayl was Borne . march . 14 . 1659 .
his Daughter margret . was Born . octobr . 23 . 1662 .
his ſonn Beniamen Newbery Born . Aprel . 20 . 1669 .
his Daughter Hanna . ye 2 . Borne . July . 1 . 1673 .

[Tho]mas orton married margret Pall . Juen . 1641 .
his ſonn John orton was Borne febury . 17 . 1647 .
his Daughter mary . was Borne . may . 16 . 1650 .
his Daughter ſara . was Baptiſed . auguſt . 22 . 1652 .
his Daughter elizabeth was Baptiſd . octob^{r} . 1 . 1654 .

John owen married Rebeca Wade . octobr . 3 . 1650 .
his ſonn Joſias ouen was Borne . ſeptm^{r} . 8 . 1651 .
his ſonn John ouen was Borne . noum^{r} . 5 . 1652 . Dead
his . 2 . ſonn John owen Borne . Aprell . 23 . 1654 . Dead
his ſonn Nathanel ouen Borne . Auguſt . 9 . 1656 .
his ſonn Daniell ouen was Born . march . 28 . 1658 .
his ſonn Joſeph ouen was Borne . octobr . 23 . 1660 .

1 This word is written in black ink.

his Daughter mary was Born . Defm[r] . 5 . 1662 .
his fonn Beniamen was Borne . feptm[r] . 20 . 1664 . Dead .
[59] Rebeca Daughter of John ouen was Borne . march . 28 . 1666 .
obedia fonn of John owen was Borne . Decmb[r] . 12 . 1662 .
Ifack fonn of John ouen was Borne . may 27 . 1670 .

John ofbon married Ann ouldag . may . 19 . 1645 .
his fonn John ofbon was Borne . Janury . 10 . 1645 .
his Daughter Ann was Borne . January . 15 . 1647 .
his fonn Nathanell was Borne . march . 10 . 164 . 9 .
his fonn famuell was Borne . July . 25 . 1652 . Dead
his Daughter mary . was Borne . Aprel . 16 . 1655 .
his Daughter Hanna was Borne . Decem[r] . 18 . 1657 .
his . 2 . fonn famuell ofbon . Borne . may . 8 . 1660 .
his fonn Ifack ofbon was Born . feptm[r] . 28 . 1664 .
his Daughter fara was Borne . febury . 8 . 1666 .
his Daughter efter was born . Aguft . 9 . 1662 .

Robard ould married fufanna Hanford . Decmbr . [31 . 1669 .]
his fonn Robard ould was Borne . octobr . 9 . 1670 .
his fonn Jonathan was Borne . January . 4 . 1672 .

John ofbon iun[r] married Abigail egelfton . octobr . 14 . 1669 .
abigal his daftr was born in march 2 wek . 71 .
mindwell his daftr was born in Janury . 2 wek . 73 .
ann his daftr was born . in Janury firft wek . 75
mary his daftr born Janury laft wek . 77

Jofias owen maried mary ofbon . october . 22 . 1674 .
his fonn Jofias was borne . Juen . 6 . 1675 .

his ſonn Iſack was borne . Juen . 4 . 1678 .
his dafter mary was born . febuary . 15th . 1679 .

[60] P . ould mr william Phelpes .
his ſonn Timothy Phelps was borne here in Aguſt . 1639 .
his Daughter mary was Borne here in march . 1644 .

---

his ſonn William Phelps married Iſabell wilſon . Juen . 4 . 1645 .
now ſinc 29 year . and has had noe child . July . 15 . 74 .

ſamuell Phelps Phelps married ſara griſwold . noumr . 10 . 1650 .
his ſonn ſamuell Phelpes was Baptiſed . ſeptemr . 5 . 1652 .
his ſonn Timothy Phelps was Borne in october . 1656 .
his Daughter ſara was Borne ye later end of march . 1653 .
his Daughter mary was Borne in october . 1658 .
his ſonn William Phelps was Born . nouembr . 3 . 1660 .
his ſonn John Phelps was borne . July . 7 . 1662 . Ded[1]
his ſonn ephraim Phlps was Born . noumr . 1 . 1663 .
his Daughter Abigayl was Borne . may . 16 . 1666 .
his ſonn Joſias Phelps was borne . Deſemr . 15 . 1667 .

ſamuell Phelps Dyed . may . 15 . 1669 .

And Nathanell Pinne maried ſara wido of ſamuel Phlps . July 21 . 1670 .
Nathanell his ſonn was borne . may ye . 11 . 1671 .
[ſara] daughter of nathanell Pinne was borne . octor . 11 . 73 .

Nathanell Phelps married Elizabeth copley . ſeptmr . 17 . 1650 .
his Daughter mary was Borne . Juen . 21 . 1651

1 This word is written in blue ink.

his ſonn Nathanell Phelps was born . Aprel . 2 . 1653 .
his Daughter Abigayl was Born . Aprel . 5 . 1655 .
his ſonn William Phelps was Born . Juen . 22 . 1657 . at northam̄t

---

Timothy Phelps marryed mary Griſwold . march . 19 . 1661 .
his ſonn Timothy Phelps was Borne . noumber . 1 . 1663 .
his ſonn Joſeph Phelps was Borne . ſeptmbr . 27 . 1666 .
his ſonn william Phelps was Borne . febury . 4 . 1668 .
his ſonn cornelus Phelps was Born . Aprel . 26 . 1671 .
his Daughter mary was Borne . Aguſt . 14 . 1673 .
his ſonn ſamuell Phelps Borne . Janury . 29 . 75 .
[61] Nathanell ſonn of Timothy Phelps was born .
January . ye 7 . 1677 .
ſara dafter of Timothy Phelps was borne . decem^{r} 27 . 1679 .

Georg Phelps married Phillup Randals Daughter
his ſonn Iſack Phelps was Borne . Aguſt . 20 . 1638 .
his ſonn Abrham Phelps was borne . Janury . 22 . 1642 .
his ſonn Joſeph Phelps was Born . Juen . 24 . 1647 .

---

his wife Died . Aprell . 29 . 1648 .

And he marryed a . 2 . frances ye wido of Thomas Deuey . noumbr 164[ ]
his ſonn Jacob Phelps was Borne . febury . 7 . 1649 .
his ſonn John John Phelps Borne . febury . 15 . 1651 .
his ſonn Nathanell Phelps . Born . Decem^{r} . 9 . 1654 [?]

Iſack Phelps married Ann Gaylar . march . 11 . 1662 .
his ſonn Iſack Phelpes was Borne . ſeptm^{r} . 10 . 1666 .

his Daughter ſara was baptiſed . July . 24 . 1670 . born . [ ]
his ſonn John Phelps . was baptiſed . Juen . 29 . 1673 .

Abraham Phelps married mary Pinne . July . 6 . 1665 .
his ſonn Abraham Phelps was Borne . march . 6 . 166 . 5 .
his ſonn Iſack Phelps was Borne . Aguſt . 5 . 1673 .

Joſeph Phelps married mary Porter . Juen . 26 . 1673 .
his daughter mary Phelps was Born . Janury . 13 . 1674 .
his daughter ſara was borne Aprell ye . 4 . 1677 . baptiſ[ ] July . 1 . 7[ ]
his ſonn Joſeph Phelps was borne decembr . 30 . 1678 . baptiſd . may 4 [ ]

[62] Joſeph Phelps ſonn of william Phelps maried Hanna nuton . ſeptm^{r} 20 . 1660 .
his ſonn Joſeph Phelps was Borne . Aguſt . 2 . 1667 .
his Daughter Hanna was Borne . febury . 2 . 1668 .

John Porter sn^{r} . came from Ingland and ſettled here in Windſor . in 1639 .
his ſonn Nathanell Porter was born here . July . 19 . baptiſed . 1640 .
his Daughter Hanna was Borne . ſeptem^{r} . 4 . baptiſed . 1642 .

---

he Dyed Aprell . 21 . 1648 .

---

his ſonn John John Porter married .
and his ſonn John Porter was Borne . Juen . 3 . 1651 . marid[1]
his Daughter mary was Borne . July . 17 . 1653 . maried
his Daughter ſara was Borne . ſeptm^{r} . 5 . 1655 . marid[1]
his ſonn James Porter was Borne . Deſem^{r} . 22 . 1657 .
his ſonn Nathanell Porter Borne . Aprell . 20 . 1660 .

1 This word is written in black ink.

his Daughter Hanna was Borne . Janury . 1 . 1662 .
his ſonn ſamuell Porter Borne . march . 5 . 1664 .
[hi]s Daughter Rebeca was Borne . march . 8 . 1666 .
[his] Daughter Heſter was Borne . may . 8 . 1669 .
[his] Daughter Ruth was Borne . Aguſt . 7 . 1671 .
[his] ſonn Hezekia Porter was Borne . nouembr . 9 . 1673 .
his ſonn Joſeph Porter was Born febu^{r} . 7 . 75 . Baptiſd . 13 . day

John Porter iun^{r} . married Joanna Gaylar . Deſembr . 16 . 1669 .
his Daughter Joanna was Borne . febury . 7 . 1670 .
his Daughter mary was Borne . nouem^{r} . 20 . 1672 .
his ſonn John Porter was Borne January . 17 . 1674 .
his Daughter ſara was Born Juen ye . 1 . 77 .
his Dafter Ann was borne aguſt . 26 . 1679 .

[63] Houmfery Pinne married in Dorcheſter mary Hull .
his ſonn ſamuell Pinne borne in Dorcheſter
his ſonn Nathanell Pinne borne here . in Decembr . 1641 .
his Daughter mary was Born . in Juen . baptiſed . 16 . 1644 . maried
his Daughter ſara was Born . noumber . 19 . 1648 .
his ſonn John Pinne was born in . octobr . bapiſd . 19 . 1651 .
his Daughter Abigayl was born . noum^{r} . 26 . 1654 .
his ſonn Iſack Pinne was Born . febury . 24 . 1663 .

ſamuell Pinne married Joyſe Biſſell . noum^{r} . 17 . 1665 .
his Daughter mary was Borne . Juen . 16 . 1667 .
his ſonn ſamuell Pinne was Born . noum^{r} . 20 . 1668 .

Nathanell Pinne marryed ſara . Phelps wido . July . 21 . 1670 .
his ſonn Nathanell Pinne was borne . may . 11 . 1671 .

Nathanell his fonn born . may . 11 . 71 .[1]
his Daughter fara was borne october . ye 11 : 1673 .

Eltewd Pomery .
his fonn meedad Pumery was Baptifed . Aguft . 19 . 1638 .
his fonn caleb . Pomery was Baptifed . march . 6 . 1641 .
his Daughter marcy was Born . in Apell, bapifed . 21 . 1644 . De[ad]
his fonn Jofua Pumery . was born, noumber, baptifd . 22 . 1646 .
his fonn Jofeph Pumery . was born Juen . baptifed . 20 . 1652 .

---

caleb Pumery married Hepfiba Baker . march . 8 . 1664 .
his Daughter Hepfiba was Born . July . 27 . 1666 .

Nicolas Palmer .
his Daughter mary was Borne . may . 3 . 1637 .
his Daughter Hanna was Borne . in octobr . bapifed . 11 . 1640 .
his fonn Timothy Palmer was Baptifed . march . 20 . 1641 .
his Daughter . elifabeth . was Borne . Aguft . 7 . 1644 .

[64] Samuell Pond and his wife fara ware married . noum^{r} . 18 . 1642 .
his fonn Ifack Pond was Borne march . 16 . 1646 . Dead
his fonn Nathanell Pond was born . defembr . 21 . 1650 . Dead[2]
his Daughter fara was Borne . febury . 11 . 1652 .
his fonn famuell Pond was Borne . march . 4 . 1648 .

Thomas Parfons married liddia Brown . Juen . 28 . 1641 .
his Daughter Bethia was Borne . may . 21 . 1642 .
his fonn Thomas Parfon was Born . Aguft . 9 . 1645 . Dead[1]

1 This line is crossed out.
2 This word is written in black ink.

his Daughter Abigayl was Borne . Janury . 21 . 1643 . Dead
his fonn John Parfons was Borne . noum^{r} . 13 . 1647 .
his Daughter marcy was Borne . July . 23 . 1652 .
his fonn ebenefer Parfon was born . may . 14 . 1655 .
his fonn famuell Parfon was Born . July . 18 . 1657 .
his fonn Jofeph Farfon was Borne may . 1 . 1661 .

Thomas Farfon Dyed . feptem^{r} . 23 . 1661 .
his sonn Thomas Dyed Decem^{r} . 14 . 1680 .

Thomas Parfon . married fara Dare . Defem^{r} . 24 . 1668 .
[his] Daughter fara was Borne . octobr . 12 . 1669 .
his Daughter Hanna was Borne . octobr . 3 . 1671 . Dead
his fonn Thomas Parfon was Borne . Janury . 2 . 1673 . Dead .
his wife dyed . Juen . 14 . 1674 .

Timothy Palmer marryed married Hanna Buell . feptm^{r} . 17 . 1663 .
his fonn Timothy Palmer was Borne . Aguft . 25 . 1664 .
his Daughter Hanna was Borne . octobcr . 3 . 1666 .
his Daughter mary was Borne . may . 14 . 1669 .
his Daughtr fara was Borne . febury . 25 . 1671 . Dead .
his fonn John Palmer was Borne . Aprell . 13 . 1673 .
his daughtr fara was born . Aprell . 12 . 1675 .
his fonn famuell was born feptem^{r} . 7 . 1677 .
his dafter martha was born . decmbr . 29 . 1679 .

[65] H . John Hodge married fufanna Deneflow . Aguft . 1 . 16[66]
his fonn John born at kilinworth . Juen . 16 . 1667 .
his fonn Thomas Hodg was Borne . febury . 13 . 1668 .
his Daughter mary . was Borne . febury . 15 . 1670 .

his ſonn Joſeph Hodg was . Borne . Deſembr . 14 . 1672 .
his ſonn Beniamen Hodg . Borne Juen . 17 . 1674 .
his ſonn Henery Hodg . borne Aguſt ye . 19 . 76 .
his ſonn william Hodg born Aprel ye 10 . 1678 .

Anthony Hoſkins marryed Jeſabel Brown . July . 16 . 1656 .
his Daughter Jeſabell was Borne . may . 16 . 1657 .
his ſonn John Hoſkins was Borne . october . 14 . 1659 .
his ſonn Robard Hoſkins . was Borne . Juen . 6 . 1662 .
his ſonn Anthony Hoſkins was Borne . march . 19 . 1663 . 64 .
his Daughter grace was Born . July . 26 . 1666 .
his Daughter Rebeca was Born . deſm[r] . 3 . 1668 . Dead .
his Daughter Jane was Borne . Aprel . 30 . 1671 .
his ſonn Thomas Hoſkins . borne . march . 14 . 1672 .
his ſonn Joſeph Hoſkins . born . febury . 28 . 1674 .

Thomas Hoſkins married Eliſabeth Birg widow . Aprell . 20 . [1653]
his ſonn John Hoſkins was Borne . may . 29 . 1654 .
Thomas Hoſkins Dyed Aprell . 13 . 1666 .
ye wido Hoſkins dyed . Decmbr . 22 . 1675 .

John Phelps maried ſara Buckland
his ſonn enock was Born . Janury . 21 . 1675 . baptiſed . ſ[ ]3 . 7[ ]
his ſonn John Phelps was Born Aprell . 12 . 1678 .
his ſonn Joſia Phelps was borne febury . ye 17 . 1679

[66] John Hiller .
his ſonn John Hiller was Borne . Juen . 3 . 1637 .
his Daughter mary was Borne . Deſembr . 25 . 1639 .
his ſonn Timothy Hiller was Born . Juen . 3 . 1642 .

his ſonn James Hiller was Born . Aguſt . 24 . 1644 .
his ſonn Andrew Hiller . noumr . 4 was Born . 1646 .
his ſonn ſimon Hiller was born . Deſemr . 25 . 1648 .
his ſonn Nathanell Hiller . was Born . Janury . 1 . 1650 .
his Daughter ſara was borne . Aguſt . 25 . 1652 .
his Daughter Abigayl was Borne . Aguſt . 21 . 1654 .
John Hiller snr . Dyed . July . 16 . 1655 .

Timothy Hall marryed ſara Barber . noumr . 26 . 1663 .
his Daughter ſara was Borne Aprel . 9 . 1665 .
his ſonn Timothy Hall was Borne . Deſemr . 12 . 1667 .
his ſonn John Hall was Borne . Aguſt . 24 . 1670 .
his ſonn Thomas Hall was Borne . Aguſt . 26 . 1672 .
his ſonn ſamuell Hall was Borne . Janury . 3 . 1673 .
his Daughter [?]s was borne . noumr . 28 . 75 . baptiſed . Decmr . 5 . ded
his ſonn Joſias was born ſeptembr . 22 . baptiſed . 29 . 78 .

John Pettebon marryed ſara egeleſton . febury . 16 . 1664 .
his ſonn John Pettebon was Borne . Deſemr . 15 . 1665 .
his Daughter ſara was Borne . ſeptmr . 24 . 1667 .
his ſonn ſtephen Pettebon Borne . octobr . 3 . 1669 .

Houmfery Prior married Ann Oſbon . nouemr . 12 . 1663 .
his ſonn John Prior was Borne . febury . 14 . 1664 .
his ſonn Danell Prior was Borne . deſemr . 19 . 1667 .

Iſack Pond marryed Hana Griffen . may . 10 . 166[7]
his Daughtr Hanna was Born . febury . 10 . 1667 .

[67] William Parſon . married Hanna Parkes . octobr : 26 . 166[6]

his ſonn William Parſon was Borne . July . 27 . 1669 .
his daftr Hanna born nouember . 3 . 78 .

R . Abraham Randell and his wife mary ware married . Decem^r^ . 8 . 1640
now . 74 . is ſenc 34 yers and had no child . his wife Died
July ye 8 . 77 . nixt decembr maied . 37 yers . [1]

John Rockwell married ſara enſigne . may . 6 . 1651 .
his Daughter ſara was Borne . may . 12 . 1653 .
his Daughter ruth was Borne . march . 5 . 1654 .
his Daughter liddia was Borne . noum^r^ . 23 . 1656 .
his wife ſara Dyed . Juen . 23 . 1659 .

---

he married a . 2 . wife Deliueranc Hayes . Aguſt . 18 . 1662 .
his ſonn John he had by hir was Borne ſeptem^r^ 5 . 1663 . Dyed
his Daughter Hanna was Borne . may . 30 . 1665 .
his ſonn Joſeph Rockwell was Born . July . 8 . 1668 .
his Daughter eliſabeth was Borne . febury . 5 . 1670 .
he Dyed ſeptember . 3 . 1673 . 46 . yer ould .

he was Born . march . 28 . 1631 .
ſamuell Rockwell married mary Norton . Aprell . 7 . 1660
his Daughter mary was Borne . Janury . 18 . 1661 .
his Daughtr Abigayle was Borne . Aguſt . 23 . 1664 . Dead[2]
his ſonn ſamuell Rockwell was Born . octo^r^ . 19 . 1667 .
his ſonn Joſeph Rockwell was Borne . may . 22 . 1670 .
his ſonn John Rockwell . was Borne . may . 31 . 1673 .
his daughter Abigall was borne aprell . 11 . 76 .
his ſonn Joſia was born march . 10 . 78 . baptiſed . ye 23 . day

1 Entry of death in black ink.
2 This word is written in black ink.

Thomas Rowly married mary Denflow . may . 5 . 69 .
his Daughter mary was Borne . Aprell . 16 . 1670 .
his Dafter martha was born . may . 13 . 1677 .
his fonn John was borne octobr . 27 . 1679 . dyed and burid noumr 10 7[ ]

[68] John Strong senor .
his Daughter elifabeth was Born in windfor . febury . 24 . 1647 .
his Daughter expernc was Born and baptifed . aguft . 4 . 1650 .
his fonn famuell and Jofeph both at a beurth Born
and Baptifed . Aguft ye 5 . 1652 .
his Daughter mary . was Borne . october . 26 . 1654 .
his Daughter Hanna was Borne . may . 30 . 1659 .
his Daughter Hefter was Borne . Juen . 7 . 1661 .

John ftrong iunr marryed mary Clark . noumr . 26 . 1656 .
his Daughter mary . was Borne . Aprell . 22 . 1658 .
his Daughter Hanna was Borne . Aguft . 11 . 1660 .

---

this his wife mary Dyed . Aprell . 28 . 1663 .
his fecond wife elizabet[1] Warrenor .
his fonn John ftrong by hir was Borne . Defemr . 25 . 1665 .
his fonn Jacob ftrong . was Borne . Aprell . 8 . 1673 .
his fonn Jofia ftrong was borne Janury . 11 at night and
baptifed ye . 12 . day . 1678 .

[Return] ftrong married fara Warham . may . 11 . 1664 .
his Daughter fara was Borne . march . 14 . 1664 .
his Daughter Abigayl was Born . march . 8 . 1666 .
his fonn Returne ftrong was Borne . febury . 10 . 1668 .

1 Mary first written; then changed in blue ink.

his Daughter elifabeth was Borne . febury . 20 . 1670 .
his fonn famuell ftrong was Borne . may . 20 . 1673 . Dyed at . 10 . weks
his Daughter Dameris was Borne July . 3 . 1674 .
his fonn famuell Born Decmbr . 27 . 75 . baptifd Janury . 2 . 75 .
Decembr . 26 . 78 . his wife dyed . being 36 . yers ould laft Aguft .

[69] Richard Saxfton marryed . fara Cook . Aprell . 16 . 164[ ]
his Daughter fara was Borne . march . 23 . 1647 .
his fonn John faxfton was Borne . march . 4 . 1649 .
his Daughter mary was Borne . febury . 27 . 1651 .
his fonn Richard faxfton was Born . march . 1 . 1654 . Dead[1]
his Daughter Patienc was Born . Janury . 28 . 1658 .
his fonn frances faxfton was Born . Janury . 17 . 1661 . Dyed may . 6 . 62
Richard faxfton dyed . may . 3 . 1662 .
his wife fara dyed . Juen . 13 . 1674 .

Henery ftilles marryed elizabeth willcockfon . Apell . 16 . 1663 .
his Daughter elifubeth was Borne . noumr . 30 . 1664 .
his Daughter margret was Borne . febury . 6 . 1666 .
his Daughter mary was Borne . feptemr . 28 . 1669 .
his Daughter mindwell . Borne . Defembr . 19 . 1671 .
his fonn famuell was Borne . may . 16 . 1674 .

Thomas ftoton married mary wadfworth . [ ]
his fonn John ftowton was Borne . Juen . 20 . 1657 .
his Daughter mary was Borne . January . 1 . 1658 .
his Daughter elifabeth was Born . noumr . 18 . 1660 .
his fonn Thomas ftowton was Born . noumr . 21 . 1662 .
his fonn famuell ftowton was Born . feptmr . 8 . 1665 .

1 This word is written in black ink.

his fonn Ifrell ftoton was Borne . Aguft . 21 . 1667 .
his Daughter Rebeca was Borne . Juen . 19 . 1673 .

Nicolas fenchou maryed his wife Ifabell . Juen . 12 . 1645 .
now . 1680 . and 35 yere laft Juen and had no child .

[70] Thomas Dewey marryed frances clark . march . 22 . 1638 .
his fonn Thomas was borne . febury . 16 . 1639 .
his fonn Jofia was Baptifed . octo . 10 . 1641 .
his Daughter Anna was Baptifed . octor . 15 . 1643 .
his fonn Ifrell was Born . feptmr . 25 . 1645 .
his fonn Jededia was Born decmbr . 15 . 1647 .
thire father Dyed . Aprel . 27 . 48 .

Jofeph fonn of Jofep gillet was born . noumr . 2 . 1664 .
elifabet dafter of Jofep gillet was borne . Juen . 12 . 1666 .
mary dafter of Jofep gillet was born . feptmr . 10 . 1667 .
Jonathan his fonn was borne aguft . 11 . 1669 .
John fonn of Jofep gillet was born . Juen . 10 . 1671 .
nathanell his fonn was borne . may . 4 . 1673 .
Hanna . daftr of Jofep gillet was borne . Janury . 30 . 74 .

John lewis his fon . famuel born Aguft ye 6 . 1677 .
Decmbr . 18 . 79 . his dafter was born . marey .

[71] T . Stephen Tery he maried in Dorchefter .
his Daughter mary was Borne ther . Defembr . 31 . 1633 .
his fonn John Tery was born here . march . 6 . 1637 .
his Daughter elifabeth was Borne . Januay . 4 . 1641 .
his Daughter Abigayl was Borne . feptmr . 21 . 1646 .

John Tery marryed elifabeth Wadefworth . noum^{r} . 27 . 1662
his Daughter elifabeth was Borne . Defembr . 16 . 1663 .
his fonn ftephen Tery was Borne . octob^{r} . 6 . 1666 .
his Daughter fara was Borne . noumbr . 16 . 1668 .
his fonn John Tery was Borne . march . 22 . 1670 . Dyed
his Daughter Rebeca was Born . Janury . 7 . 1671 . Dead
his Daughter mary was Born . July . 19 . 1673 . Dead[1]
follomon his fonn was Born . march ye 29 . 75 . Dead[1]
his Daughter Rebeca born . febury . 27 . 76 .

Peter Tilton married his wife elifabeth . may . 10 . 164[ ]
his Daughter elifabeth was Borne . Juen . baptifed . 19 Day . 16[ ]
his Daughter mary was . baptifed . febury . 18 . 1643 .
his fonn Peter Tilton . was Borne . Decembr . 5 . 1647 .

Timothy Trall was Borne . July . 25 . baptifed . 1641 .
Timothy Trall married Debro gunn . noum^{r} . 10 . 1659 .
his Daughter Debroa was Borne . Aguft . 19 . 1660 .
his fonn Timothy Trall was Born . Defem^{r} . 7 . 1662 .
his Daughter mehettabell was Born . march . 1664 .
his Daughter elifabeth was Born . may . 1 . 1667 .
his fonn John Trall was Born . Juen . 8 . 1669 . Dead
his . 2 . fonn John Trall born . Juen . 5 . 1671 .
his Daughter martha was born . may . 31 . 1673 .
[72] Timothy Tralls fonn Thomas borne may . 5 . 75 . Dead
his 2 fonn Thomas Trall . borne . July . 10 . 1676 .

Stephen Taylar marred fara Hofford . noumber . 1 . 1642 .
his fonn ftephen Taylar was Borne . march . 11 . 1644 .

1 This word is written in black ink.

his fonn famuell Taylar was Borne . octobr . 8 . 1647 .
his fonn John Taylar was Borne . march . 22 . 1652 .
his fonn Thomas Tailas was Borne . octobr . 5 . 1655 .
his Daughter Abigayl was Borne . march . 19 . 1657 . 58 .
his Daughter mary was Borne . Juen . 18 . 1661 .
his fonn Nathanell Taylar . Born . may . 24 . 1668 .
his daughter mindwell was borne . nouember . 5 . 1663 .

Jofep Baker was born Juen . 18 . 1655 . and maried
H[a]nna wido of Thomas Buckland . but dauter of nathanell
cook . born feptem^r . 21 . 55 . and maried to Jofep baker
January . 30 . 76 . his fonn Jofep was borne . aprel . 13 . 78 .
his daughter Lidia was born . July . 5 . 1681 .

[73] owen Tudor marryed mary fkiner wido . noum^r . 13 . 16[ ]
his fonn famuel and Daughter fara born both at a berth . noum^r . 26 . 16[ ]
his fonn owen Tudor was Borne . march . 12 . 1654 .
his Daughter Jane was Borne . octobr . 16 . 1657 .
his Daughter mary was Born . march . 6 . 1660 .

Aguft . 19 . his wife dyed . buried ye 20 . day . 1680 .

m^r John warham his firft child born here of his wife Jane
was his Daughter Abigyl . Baptifed may . 27 . 1638 .
his Daughter Hepfiba . baptifed aguft . 9 . 1640 . D[ead]
his Daughter fara Borne . aguft . 28 . 1642 .
his Daughter Hefter . Baptifed . Defem^r . 8 . 164[4]

---

his wife Jane dyed . at norwake Aprel [ ]3 . 16[ ]5 .
he married m^st Abigayl Branker wido . octo^r . 9 . [1662]

m^r John Warham Dyed . Aprell . 1 . 1670 .

---

m^r Henery wolcot married fara Newbery . nou[m . 1]8 [1641]
his fonn Henery wolcot was Born . bapaptifed . January 8 . 1642[1]
his fonn John wolcot was Born febury . baptifed . march [2] 1644[1]
his Daughter fara was borne . July . 1649
his Daughter mary was Baptifed . Decem . 7 . 1651 .
his Daughter Hanna was Borne . march . 7 . 1653 .
his fonn famuell wolcot was Born . Aprel . 16 . 1656 .
his fonn Jofias was Borne . July . 21 . 1658 .
m^r wolcot sn^r . dyed . July . 12 . buried ye 13 . day . 1680 .

[74] Henery wolcot iun^r married Abia goffe . octobr . 12 . 1664 .
his Daughter elifabeth was Borne . Aguft . 27 . 1665 .
his fonn Henery wolcot was Born . Aprell . 13 . 1667 . Dyed .
his Daughter Abiah was Borne . may . 1 . 1669 .
his Daughter fara was Born . march . 27 . 1671 . Dead[2]
his fonn . Henery wolcot . Borne . march . 30 . 1673 .
his 2 daughter fara borne Aprel . 16 . 76 .
his fonn famuell was Born march . 26 . 1679 . baptifed 30 . day

[S]imon wolcot married martha Pitkin . octobr . 17 . 1661 .
[h]is Daughter elifabeth . was Borne . aguft . 19 . 1662 .
[his]Daughter martha was Borne . may . 17 . 1664 .
[his] fonn fimon wolcot . was Born . Juen . 24 . 1666 .
[his D]aughter Joanna . was Born . Juen . 30[3] . 1668 .
his fonn Danell borne in aguft 1676 .
his fonn Roger borne January . 28 . 1678 .

---

1 This date has been written over in a modern hand.
2 This word is written in blue ink.
3 First written Aguft 7 and crossed out.

Robard watſon marryed mary Rockwell . Defemr . 10 . 1646 .
his Daughter mary was Borne . Janury . 11 . 1651 .
his ſonn John watſon was Borne . march . 7 . 1653 .
his ſonn ſamuell watſon . Borne . Janury . 14 . 1655 .
his Daughter Hanna was Borne . Aguſt . 8 . 1658 .
his ſonn ebenezer was Borne . Aprell . 25 . 1661 .
his ſonn Nathanel watſon . Born . Janury . 28 . 1663 .
his ſonn Jededia watſon . Born . ſeptemr . 30 . 1666 .

[75] Richard weller married Ann Wilſon . ſeptmr . 17 . 16[ ]
his Daughter Rebeca was Born . may . 10 . 1641 .
his Daughter ſara was Borne . Aprel . 10 . 1643 .
his ſonn John weller was Baptiſed . Aguſt . 10 . 1645 .
his ſonn Nathanell weller Borne . July . 15 . 1648 .
his ſonn eliaſor weller . Borne . noumr . 20 . 1650 .
his ſonn Thomas weller . Borne . Aprel . 10 . 1653 .

Robard winchell . his children born here ware
his Daughter Phebe was Baptiſed . march . 29 . 1639 .
his Daughter mary . was Baptiſed . ſeptemr . 5 . 1641 .
his ſonn Dauid winchell . Baptiſed . october . 22 . 1643
his ſonn Joſeph winchel . Baptiſed . Aprel . 5 . 1646
his Daughter martha Baptiſed . Juen . 18 . 1648 .
his ſonn Beniamen . Baptiſed . July . 11 . 1652 .
Robard winchell Dyed . January . 21 . 1667 .

Nathanell winchell marryed ſara Porter . Aprel [8 . 1664]
his ſonn Nathanell winchell was Borne . Aguſt . 5 . 1665 .
his ſonn Thomas winchell was Borne . may . 25 . 166[ ]
his Daughter ſara was borne Decembr . 26 . 1674 .

his ſonn ſtephn born Aguſt 13 . 1677 .

Jonathan Winchell marryed Abigayl Brunſon . may . 16[66]
his ſonn Jonathan winchell was Borne . febury . 166[7] .

Dauid winchell marryed Eliſabeth ffilly . noum^r^ . 17 . 1669 .
his ſonn Joſeph winchell was Borne . ſeptem^r^ . 13 . 1670 .
his daughtr chriſtan was borne march . 9 . 1672 .
his daughter eliſabeth was borne decmb^r^ . 9 . 1675 .

[76] John Williams marryed mary Burlly . Juen . 29 . 1644 .
his ſonn John williams was Borne . march . 26 . 1646 . Dead
his ſonn Nathanell williams . Borne . october . 25 . 1647 .
his Daughter Rebeca was Borne . Aprel . 20 . 1649 .
his Daughter Hanna was Borne . Aprell . 13 . 1651 . Dead[1]
his Daughters mary and eliſabeth Both at a berth Janr . 5 . 1652 .
his Daughter Abiell was Born . ſeptm^r^ . 2 . 1655 .
his Daughter Abigayle was borne may . 31 . 1658 .

Nicolas wilton married mary ſtanniford . moum^r^ . 20 . 1656 .
his ſonn Dauid[2] wilſon was Borne . January . 13 . 1660 .
his ſonn John[3] wilſon was Born Aguſt . 8 . 1664 .

[J]ohn ſhare married ſara gibbes . Deſem^r^ . 5 . 1661 .
[his] ſonn John ſhare was Borne . Deſembr . 11 . 1662 .

John Williams and Bethia maſkell wido both ware
married by Capten Newbery . Aguſt . 8 . 1672 .
frances ſonn of John Williams was Borne . may . 25 . 1673 .

1 This word is written in black ink.
2 First written John and crossed out.
3 First written Nicolas and crossed out.

alfo John ye firſt born and ebenezr ye 2
both at a berth fonns of John Williams was
borne January ye 7 . 1675 .

Joſua welles & Afubath Lamſon waried by capten Newbery
may . 5 . 1670 . his fonn Jonathan was borne . decmbr . 24 . 70 .

[77] & mary grifen maried
ſamuell[1] ſonn[1] of[1] ſamuell wilſon was Born[1] . may . 1 . 1672 .
Jezabell daufter of ſamuell wilſon was Borne . febury . 24 . 73 .
mary daughter of ſamuell wilſon was Born . Aguſt . 5 . 1675 .
Thomas fonn of ſamuell wilſon . born . July . 18 . baptiſed . 23 . 1676 .[2]
his fonn ſamuell was born . nouembr . 21 . 1678 .

John Petebon & fara egelſt ware maried . 16 febr . 1664 .
his fonn John was borne decmr . 15 . 1665 . his dafter fara was
borne . ſeptmr . 24 . 1667 . his fonn ſtephn . borne . octor . 3 . 1669

maried his firſt wif . Juen . 4 . 1645 .
William Phelps maried fara Pinne . Decmr . 20 . 1676 .

John ſaxſton maried mary Hill . July . 30 . 1677 .

Abigall Daughter of ebenezr Parſons . born . aguſt . 1 . 75 .
ebenezr fonn of ebenezr Parſons . borne . aprel . 16 . 77 .
John fonn of ebenezer Parſons . borne . July . 29 . 78 .

[78] Thomas Debell iunr . maried mary Tucker . ocobr . 10 . 1676 .
mary Tucker born in Ingland . octobr . 4 . 1653 .

1 These words are crossed out.
2 This entry is crossed out.

his ſonn Thomas Debll . was born Aguſt . 21 . 1677 .
July . 30 . 79 . a ſecond ſonn born dead .
his Daftr mary born . aguſt . 9 . 1680 .

John Higly & Hanna Drak ware maried . noum^r^ . 9 . 71 .
his ſonn Jonathan was Borne febry . 16 . 1675 . baptisd . 20 .
his daughter Hanna was born march . 13 . 1677 . baptiſed ye 17 . day dead
his ſonn John born . Aguſt . 16 . 1673 Aguſt . 7 . 1679 .
his dafter Ketren borne .

Samuell ffarmworth of Dorcheſter in ye bay and Mary dauter
of Thomas ſtoton of windſor ware maried . Juen . 3 . 77 .
his Daughter mary was borne . may . 17 . 1678 . and dyed ye . 26 . day

Nathanell gaylar twenty to yers olld maried Abigal
Daughtr of Thomas Biſſell . 20 . yer old . octo . 17 . 78 . marid
Hezecia his ſonn was borne Aguſt . 23 . 1679 .

John Hiller his Dafter eliſabeth was borne Decembr ye . 8 . 1680 .
his dafter Ann was born may ye 8 . 1677 . and dyed . July . 17 . 8[ ]

[79] ſuſanna Daughter of m^r^ criſtophar ſanders was
borne noumb^r^ . 20 . 1676 .
his ſonn Danell ſanders was Born . octo^r^ . 27 . 1678 .
his daughter elizabeth . was born tuſday . 30 . of aguſt . 1681 .

Anna daughter of Joſep loomys ſonn of John loomyes
was born Janury . 10 . baptiſed ye 12 day . 1678 .

James Hillar maried ye wido that was wife of
ebenzer Debell Juen . 28 . 77 .

his ſonn James was Born January . 28 . 1678 ded
his dafter eliſabeth was Born . may . 6 . 80 ..

Nathanell Bancroft and Hanna daftr of John williams
ware married by capten Newbery dember . 26 . 1677 :
John ſonn of Nathnell Bancroft was Born . Janry .. 24 . 78
his ſonn Nathanell was born . ſeptm[r] . 25 . 1680 .

[80] Joſia Barber maryed Abigall daughter of Nahanell
Loomys by capten Newbery . noumber ye 22 . 1677 .
his dafter Abigall was borne march . ye 12 . 1678 .

Job ſonn of Job Drake was maried to eliſabeth Cook wido
that was Danell clarks daughter . ſeptembr . 13 . 1677 .
his ſonn Job was borne January[1] octobr . 26 . 1678 .
his daughter mary was born . Aprell . 29 . 1680 .

Thomas Newbury and Ann ford ware maried . march . 12 . 76 .
his ſonn Thomas was borne Janury . 20 . 1677 . Dyed . feb[r] . 11 . 80 .
his dafter Hanna was Borne febuary . 10 . 1679 .

may . 6 . 79 . goodman oſmer of Hartford and ye wido wilton, that had
Bin wife to Daued wilton ware to be maried at Hartford .

[81] Cornelus gillet his formar plac being full has here entred
Juen . 30 . 79 . his ſonn Danell was born . July . 27 . was baptiſed .

Thomas Burnam iun[r] and Naomy Hull ware maried at killing wort
January . 4 . 1676 . his ſonn Thomas was borne . aprel . 16 . 1678 .
his ſonn John was borne . may ye . 22 . 1681 .

1 This word is crossed out.

John Hofkines and Debro Deneflo ware marryed . Janury . 29 . 1677 .
his Daftr elifabeth[1] was born . Juen . 9 . 1679 . baptifed . octo[r] . 19 . 79 .

Thomas fonn of Thomas Biffell sn[r] was maried to efte[ ]
dafter of John ftrong elder . at norhamton . octob[r] . 15 . 1678 .
his dafter efter was borne feptemb[r] . ye 10 . 1679 .
baptifed ye 5 of octobr . 79 . baptifed . octo[r] . 19 . 79 .[2]
his dafter Abigall was born . octobr . 26 . 1681 .

[82] John Hodg and fufanna Denflo Dafter of Henery
Denflo . ware maried . Aguft . 1 . 1666 .
Thomas fonn of John Hodg was born . febry . 13 . 1668 .
marey dafter of John Hodg was born . febry . 15 . 1670 .
beniamen fonn of John Hodg was born . Juen . 17 . 1674 .
william fonn of John Hodge was Born . aprel . 10 . 1678 .
John Hog has mor childrn as may be fen, 8 leus before befor
anthony Hofkins which I did know befor I began her .

William goren fonn of Henery goren was
Borne october ye 13 day . 1679 .

E Jofias fonn of Jofias elefworth . and martha gaylar
daughter of famuell gaylar ware maried . octo[r] . 30 . 79 .
Jofia 24 . yer old . martha in hir . 20 . yer .
his Daughter martha was born octobr ye . 5 . 1680 .

G Danell fonn of cornelus gillet was borne . Juen . 30 .
1679 . and baptifed . July . 27 . 79 .

---

1 Debra has been crossed out.
2 This second entry of baptism is crossed out.

[83] James fonn of James enno was maried to Abigall
dafter of famuell Biffell decembr . . 26 . . 1678 .
his fonn James was Borne . feptm[r] . 23 . 1679

James fonn of John Portr sn[r] . and fara Tuder ware mar
ried by m[r] wolcot . January . ye 15 . 1679 .
James . fonn of James Portr was borne . octobr . . 13 . 1680 . dyed January . 14 . . 80

John Birg and Hanna watfon maried . march . 28 . 1678 .
his fonn John Birg was born . febury . 4 . 1679 .

James Enno iner . his firft wifife dyed . octo . 7 . 1679 . and he maried a nother . Hefter that was ye wif of James egelfton . aprl . 29 . 1680

[84] Mical Taintor and mary daftor of Thomas loomys
ware married . Aprell ye 3 . 1679 .
his fonn mical was borne feptember ye . 6 . 1680 .

Thomas Powell & Alfe Traharn maried . 25 aguft . 1676 .
his dafter ann was borne . aprell . 19 . 1678 .
his fonn Thomas Powell . was borne . July . 11 . 1680 .

Jofeph fkiner and marey filley ware maried
aprell ye 5 . 1666 : his dafter mary was borne fept . 22 . 67 .
his dafter elifabeth was borne : January : 23 : 1669 .

Jofia gillet & Johana Tainter ware maried by m[r] John Allyn .
Juen . 30 . 1676 . Jofias fonn of Jofias gillet was borne noum[r] . 24 . 78 .
Johanna dafter of Jofias gillet was born . octobr . 28 . 1680 .

[85] Beniamen Egelſton and hanna ye widow ſhadock ware
maried by capten newbery . march ye 6 . 1678 .
his daughter marcy was born . 2 october . 1680 .

Joſias owen maried mary oſbon . october . 22 . 1674 .
thire

Enock Drak maried ſara Porter . noumbr . 11 . 1680 both 25 yere
ould . ſara . 5 of laſt Juen enock ye 8 of nixt month
thire dafter ſara born . tuſday . may . 31 . 1681 .

Samuell Biſells ſonn John . maried Abigall dafter of willi
am filly . Agust . 26 . 1680 . he 20 . yer . ould . 5 . of laſt aprel
his wif . 22 . ye 21 of laſt aguſt
his dafter abigall was borne Aguſt ye 3 . 1681 .

Nathanel ſon of Nathanell loomys was maried Elizabeth Elſ
worth Decm^{r} . 23 . 1680 . he 24 . yer ould ye 20 . of nixt march
ſhe 23 . yer old ye 11 . of laſt noumbr .

Danell ſon of John loomis maryed, maried mary Elezwo[ ]
Decmb^{r} 23 . 1680 . he 23 yere ould ye 16 . of laſt Juen . ſhee wa[s]
20 . yere ould laſt may ye 7 .

[86] Aguſt . 17 . 77 . I find in an ould book .
that march . 10 . 1638 . it was reckned
from ye begining of ye plantation
hether to that there has dyed of ould
and young . 27 . but not thire
names exprſt . but 2 that ware
members and ye captens wife

Aprel . 3 . 1639 .
ye wife of Joſep clark
dyed .
may . 16 . 39 . 2 childrn dyed
John Phelps . Thomas
fenchon .
Juen . 7 . 39 . pamers child

of children 16 . of ſeruants . 8 .
14 march . 2 youths drwned being
in a canno one ye flood gathring
vp of palles ſwiming on ye flood
againeſt Thomas Deweys hows
mathew rainend . Henery luſh .

---

and that there had bin borne of
children from ye begining to this
time . 40 . but haue not thire names

And that ye great flood began one
ye 5 . of march . one ye 11 of march
it began to fall . but by reaſon of much
rayne one ye 12 day it roſe very hoy
on ye 15 . 16 . day it had fallen nere
2 foot . but on ye 16 day was much
raine and great wind out of ye ſou
th eaſt which made it an exceding great
ſtorme, it indangred Howſes and brak
downe many trees . ſo that by ye cauſe of
which raine all ye 17 an 18 day ye waters
roſe verey hoy more then euer had bin
knowen by ye Indans . it drowned ma
ny howſes verey deep . and in dangred
cattell ouſer ye riuer for all ye ground
there was drowned to one littell ridg whe
re ſamuell grant now liues . it caried
a way much timber & haye . it beat up
palls out of ye ground and poſts and rayles

July . 8 . Thomas ſonn
born . 9 day dyed .
Auguſt 25 . John Hulbard
dyed .
ſeptemr . [10] 39 . young
mathew grant dyed .
octobr . 20 . priſſila mar
ſhfild dyed .
decmr . 3 . goode buell
dyed .

Juen . 10 . 1640 . ſamuel
roſeter . dyed .
Juen . 23 . John dewey
drouned in ye r:et
auguſt . 22 . eliſabet
gunn dyed .
auguſt . 25 . Joſias
Terey dyed .
ſeptmr . 5 . mr clar
kes ſiſter dyed .
ſeptmr . 18 . Joanna
Hofford dyed .
ſeptmr . 23 . Abigal
carter dyed .
octo . 7 . Ann maſ
ſen . dyed .
decmr . 17 . ſtephen
Tery dyed .
decemr . 19 . mary

and caried them a way, and holl trees
and all . on ye 18 day at night there was
great feare of another ſtorme . of wind
and rayne it began but it pleaſed ye
lord it ſeaſſed quickly and by ye mor
ning one might perſaue ye water was
be gan to fall and ſo it continued . one
ye 22 day at night it was well fallen &
yet it was as hoye as ye hoyeſt flood
we had knowen before .

---

aguſt . 17 . 1639 . mr Hweit and diures
others came up from ye bay to windſor
to ſettell heer

Pumery dyed .
febuay . 11 . roberd
wilton d[ied]

---

m[a]y [ye?] . 29 . 164[o the]
mother mathew gr
ant . dyed .
may . 31 . ſamuel
deble buried .

[87] [M]ay . 23 . 76 : A count of Parſons that haue dyed in [ ]
to [be]gin .

ye 40 yere . 2 . Parſons
william Rockwell
Henery fookes .

---

41 year . 4 . Parſons .
Joſeph clark .
giles Gibbes .
John Biſſells wife .
William Horſfords wife .

---

ye 47 . year . 27 . Parſons . dyed
ſtephen Terys wife
Hepsiba waram[1]
Joſua carter .
John Porters snr . wife .
caleb carter .
Richard Beddell .
gorg Phelps child
ſamuell warham
Hoytes child .

1 This name is interlined in very small letters. It, as well as the same name eight lines below, and the figure 7 two lines above, is in ink of a darker shade from other entries on the page. The number of deaths was first written 26 and the seven written later over the six. The lower of the two names seems to be traced over the same name previously written in the lighter ink.

4[2 yea]re . 3 Farfon .
Tho[ ]rds wife[1] .
John Grifwold
fara Hueit
Nathanel Hueit

---

43 . year . 5 . Parfons .
Thomas fords wife .
John burg .
abigal fylar .
anna Rockwell .
richard birg a child .

---

44 . yer . 8 . Parfons .
mr Huiet
ould goode Hayt .
John Tomfons child
rafe newman .
mary Tery .
one Hager .
ye wido webfter
anna Taylar

---

45 . year . 4 . Parfons .
roger williams wife .
Thomas moore
gorg Patrum .
fufana Hueit .
Hepfiba warham
Thomas Bafcoms child .
Samuell Pond . 2 children dyed
fara Hayward
fara fenchon
gorg Phelps another child
marcy Hayward
Thomas Thornton .
gorg Allixanders child
John orton
goodman bidw[ ][2]
fufauna Hanum
Anthony Howkins child
Priffila Thornton
Ann Thornton
Henery curtices child
Timothy Rofeter
John Pumery .

---

48 . yeare . 25 Parfons
John Porter senr . dyed
Thomas Dewey .
famuell Allyen .
gorg Phelps his wife .
John Hofkines
Danell clarks child
famuell Allins child
benidict Aluard : 3 childrn dye[ ]

1 This line is crossed out.
2 The name was first written good man Biddel and crossed out.

---

46 year . 6 . Parſons .
nicolas Palmers wife .
mihell Tryes wife .
nicolas oumſteds child .
nathan Gillets child
John egelſton .
ſamuell fylar .
Henery wolcots child
richard ſammais child
roſe Porter
ephram bartlet
James enno . 2 children
Phillup Randall died
abigayl Phelps .
abigayl Gillet .

---

in thes . 7 years aboue
ye Parſones dyed
are . 32 .

[88] edward chakwell
Thomas Nowell dyed
Thomas orton . 2 childrn
Abigayl roſeter
Thomas Holcoms child

---

49 . yeare . 3 . Parſons .
Samuell cooke
efter Roſeter
ſtephen fylar

---

50 . yere . 4 . Parſons .
Richard ſamways dyed
mary Hayward
Hanna Taylar
Johanna fylar

---

ye wife of richard w[ell]er
martha winchell died
ye wife of anthony Howkins
nathan gillet a ſon & dauter .
Daniell Hoyte dyed
John Hiller snr dyed .
Peter Tiltons daughter
ye wife of william Hayden .

---

56 . 4 . Parſons dyed
beniamen winchell
Jonathan Holcom
ye ſon of John g[ay]lar
william Gaylar dyed .

---

57 . year . 9 . Parſons dyed .
marcy Pumery

51 . yeere . 5 . Parſons
Peter R[oset]er
Richard [Bu]rg dyed
Henery ſtiles by a gunn
elizabeth Roſeter
Joana Deble

ſara ſtowton dyed
Joſph loomys snr . his wife
John williams daughter
52 yere theſ 3 . Parſons

---

53 yeare . 3 . Parſons dyed
ye wife of william Gaylar iunr
[E]lias & eliſha carter

---

54 . year . 4 . Parſons dyed
ſara dautr of Joſep loomys
Thomas ſon of Thomas loomys
ſara Holcom
ſamuell Pond dyed .

---

55 year . 17 . Parſons
Henery wolcot senor
Thomas gunnes dautr elizabt
Nicolas Hoyts wif dyed
eltwed Pumerys wife
Nicolas Hayt dyed
ye wife of Henry wolcot eldr
Jefery Baker died
ye wife of ſimon milles
ye wife of william Gaylr snr
ye wife of walter Gaylar
Thomas Holcom dyed .
efter Hayward
marcy egelſton .
mary buckland
ye wife of James enno .

---

58 . yere . only Joſeph loomys senr .

---

59 . year . 9 . Parſons .
mr witchflds wife dyed .
Joſep clarke dyed .
Iſack Hakes druned .
ye wife of John rokwell
ye wife of ſimon milles .
ye wife of william wadſwort
John Drake senr
abigall Parſons
Thomas Allyns ſon John

---

ye 60 . yere . 2 Parſons
ketron Gibbs : Richard oldag .

---

61 . yere . 6 . Parſons .
Thomas ſtoton snr . dyed
mst huiet dyed
ſamuel milles . & ſara loomys .
rafe ſmith & Thomas Farſon

ye wife of robard winchell

[89] 62 yeare . 16 . Parſons .
ye wife of Thomas loomys
richard ſaxſton .
Phillup randall
frances ſaxſton
John Rockwell snr
wilmot his wife
wife of gorg Phillups
Pheby winchell
mr Branker .
Thomas Buckland
John ſtilles
John Brancroft
chriſtopher wolcott
ye wife of Thomas Barber
Thomas Barber
ould wido Hoſkins .

---

63 . year . 3 . parſons
ye wife of John ſtrong .
Hanna Nubery .
ye ſon of John rockwell .

---

64 . yere . 4 . Parſons .
Job Draks ſon . Joſep
Timoty ſon of Tim bukland

---

47 to ye end of 61 . ye numbr
of Parſons dyed ar 121 .

68 . yeare . only . 1 . Parſon
Jeremy burg .

Samuell Phelpes .
mst witchfeld .
James riſings wife
ould wido Denſlow . 84 . ould
John ſhare : Iſack Pond .
John loomys ſon . James .

---

thes 6 . Parſons died in
69 . yere .

---

70 . yere . 7 . Parſons
mr warham dyed
John Bartlet . ebenzr Debles
Dafter . John Terys ſon .
ſon . of John owen .
mr mathew Allyn .
ye wif of nathan gillet .

---

71 . yere . 2 . Parſons
Henery wolcots daughter
Thomas maſkell .

---

mr william Phelps .

mathew of Tahan grant .
Jacob of Jacob Gibbs .

---

65 . yere . 9 . Parſons .
ye wife of John Biſſell snr
fonn of John owen
daughtr of ſamuel rockwl
ſimon Rockwell .
Dauid ſon . of John loomys .
mary of edward chapman
eſay bartlet .
John williams iunr
ould wido Randall . 87 . old .

---

66 . yere . 4 Parſons
mary Janes & wif of m[1] grant
nico[las] maybee .
nicolas Denſlow . 90 . old

---

67 . yere . 4 . Parſons
Henery wolcots ſon & Jos . gaylr
ſam . fillys ſon . & rob . winc[hel]
nathanel Biſſells ſon .
Thomas loomys ſon .
Joſep griſwold .
nicolas Bucklands ſon .

---

thes . 5 . Parſons dyed in
72 .

---

73 . yere . 13 . Parſons
ye widow fox
Decon Gaylar . 88 . ould
returnes ſtrongs ſon .
ye wife of John fitch
John Rockwell . Dyed
3 children buried on day .
ſun of John oſbon snr & fonn
of Zurobal fylar .
dautr of nathanl Biſſell
dafter of anthony Hoſkins
dautr of John Tery .

---

74 . yere . 6 . Parſons
James Riſings wife
wido ſaxſtone .
Thomas Parſons wife
begat egelſton
John ſtiles wife .
nicol[as] bukl[and] daftr

---

1 The m stands for Matthew, the writer of the record. See his family record as copied in Stiles, vol. II, p. 304.

[90] 75 . yeare . 12 [Perfons]
John befum druned
John loomys daughtr .
Danell Haydns fon .
old m^st allyn
william Phelps wife
ye wido Hofkins
nicolas Buckland fon
famuell marfhal in war
edward chapman . war
ebenzr Deble in war
nathanel Pond in war
richard faxfton in war

---

62 . to ye eand of . 75 .
are . 91 . parfons .
& . 153 . all . 244 . Parfons

---

76 lida Howard
John fitch
fon of John Lewis
fon of abrm deble
famul barbrs wif
Thomas rulye child
lidia cook
mefngrs dafter
Thomas bukland
gorg fandrs child
elias fhadok

efter dafter of Thomas[1]
Biffel dyed . may . 9 . 7[8] .

Thomas fon of Jonathan
gillet dyed . Juen . 11 . 78 .
a 11 days ould .

---

gorg Phillups . dyed . July ye
9 . 78 .

Ifrell dewey dyed octo^r
23 . 1678 .

---

fara wif of Return ftr
ong dyed . Decm^r . 26 . 1678

---

m^r witchfild dyed march . 16 .
78 . on fabat day morning .
buried ye 18 . day .

Wiliam Trall dyed Aguft
ye 3 . fabath day . 1679 . 73 . ould

Decmbr . 2 . 79 . James egel
ftone dyed ye euening [b]e
fore and buried that day .

---

famul gaylrs wif dyed may
2 . 1680 .

---

1 The remaining records on this page appear to have been written at different times.

famul gibbs Daftr
Thomas bifels fon
william Trals wif
Timoty Trals fon
nathanl pinne
Jofua welf . wife
John brooks wif
Hana Buklands child
all are . 19 .

---

77 . William fonn of John
layton dyed . may . 7 .
ye wife of Abraham
Randall dyed . July . 8 .
aguft 23 . 77 . Jonathan
gillet sn^r dyed .
ezekia gaylar dyed
feptem . 12 . 1677 .

Decon moore dyed
feptem^r . 18 . 1677 .
John bifell sn^r dyed
octob^r . 3 . 77 .
John Terys fonn
falomon dyed . octo^r . 27 . 77 .

---

ye wife of John williams dyed
aprel 18 . 1681 .

---

mary ye wife of Jofeph loomys
dyed . Aprel 22 . 1681 .

---

ye wife of Thomas Deble sen^r
dyed . may 14 . 1681 .

---

ye ould widow Buckland dyed
July . 26 . 1681 .

[91] This is ye count of what Parfons gaue to ye uollintari con trebution mad for ye Poor in wanths in other collonyes .
upon a motion fent to This collony of conecticot it was don
Juen . 11 . 76 .

	Name	Amount
A.	mr T . Allyn	0—6—6
	benidic Aluard	0–10—0
	Jeremy Aluard	0—1—3
	Joſias [ ]lu[ ]d	0—2—6
	edward Admes	0—0—7
B	John Biſſill sn .	0—2—0
	John Biſſell iunr	0—5—0
	Thomas Biſſell	1—0—0
	Na[t]hanell Biſſell .	1—0—0
	Samuell Biſſell	0—4—0
	John Brooks	0—1—0
	Beniamn Bartlet	0—1—0
	nicolas Buckland	0—2—6
	Joſep Birg	0—3—0
	Samuell Baker	0—2—6
	Thomas Barber	0—1—0
	Peter Brown	0—9—7
	Sara Buell . siluer	0—1—0
	Joſias Barber	0—2—6
	Ephram Bancraft	0—1—6
	William Buell	0—1—3
C	mr chancy	1—0—0
	widow chapman	0–10—6
	ſamuell croof	0—2—6
	nathanell cook	0—1–10
	captin clark	0—5—0
	James Corniſh	0—5—0
	gabrel Corniſh	0—1—3
	nathanel cook iunr . & ſiſtr .	0—1—3
	Jams egelſton	0—1—6
f	Waltr fylar	0—8—0
	John fylar	0—2—6
	Zurobl fylar	0—1—3
	ſamuel forward	0—1—3
	William filly	0—0—7
	Samuel filly	0—5—0
	John filley	0—2—6
G.	Jonathan Gillet snr	0—4—6
	nathan Gillet	0—2—6
	cornelus Gillet	0—2—6
	nicolas Godard	0—2—6
	Joſep griſwold	0—2—6
	Jonathan gillet iunr	0—2—6
	gorg Griſwold	0—3—9
	Joſias gillet	0—2—6
	John gillet	0—1—3
	mathew Grant silur	0—3—0
	Samuell Grant	0—5—0
	Tahan Grant	0—8—0
	John Grant	0—2—6
	Waltel gaylar	0—2—6
	his wife in cloth	0—6—3
	his ſon eliezer . flax	0—1—6
	John gaylar snr	0—2—6
	John gaylar iunr	0—3—0
	nathanel gaylar	0—2—0
	Joſep griſwolds wife	0—2—6
	Jacob gibbs	0—2—0
	ſamuell Gibbs	0—3—0

	eliacem cok iun	o—2—6
D	Job Drak sn[r]	o—5—6
	Jacob Drak	o—8—o
	Job Drak iun[r]	o—3—o
	John Drak iun[r]	o—3—9
	Job his brother	o—1—3
	lidia his ſiſter	o—o—6
	Iſrel Dewey	o—4—o
	his wife	o—4—o
	Thomas Debl sn[r]	o—1—3
	abram Deble	o—1—3
	John Denſlos wif ſlx .	o—o—9
e	Joſias eleſwort	o—3—o
	wido egelſton . cloth	o—4—o
	Thomas egelſton	o—2—6
[92]	Joſep loomys iun[r]	o—1—3
	John lundon	o—2—6
	his wife	o—o—9
m	Decon moor	o—6—6
	John moore iun[r]	o—4—o
	John moſſes	o—5—6
	ſimon mills	o—2—6
	Peter mills	o—1—3
	mary madeſly	o—7—6
	mary marſhall	o—8—6
n	m[s]trs newbery	o—2—6
o	John ouen	o—1—o
	ſamuell oſbon	o—1—3
P	gorg Phelpes	o—4—6
	Humfrey Pinne	o—2—o
H	Robard Hayward	o—5—o
	Timothy Hall	o—2—6
	andrew Hillar	o—2—6
	ephram Haward	o—2—6
	Hanna Higly	o—1—3
	John Hofford	o—1—6
	John Hoſins	o—1—o
l	John loomas	o—6—o
	and in mony	o—5—9
	Danel loomys	o—1—o
	Thomas loomas	o—2—6
	nathanel loomys	o—5—o
T	ſtephen Taylar sn[r]	o—5—o
	ſtephen Taylar iun[r]	o—4—o
	ouen Tudor	o—6—7
	ſamuell Tudor	o—4—o
	William Trall	o—2—6
	Timothy Trall	o—2—6
	Jude T[ru]mbell	o—1—3
	Hanna Trumal	[o]—1—3
V	richard Vore	o—1—3
W.	m[r] Wolcot	o-10—o
	m[r] H . Wolcot iun[r]	o—5—o
	Samuell Wolcot	o—5—o
	Robard Watſon	o—8—o
	Dauid Winchell	o—2—6
	nicolas Wilton	o—1—8

	fara Pinne	0—1—3
	gorg Phillups bakn	0—2—9
	John Porter sn[r]	0–10—0
	John Porter iun[r]	0—3—0
	nathanel Porter	0—1—0
	James Porter	0—2—6
	Timothy Phelps	0—3—6
	Thomas Puell[1]	0—4—0
	Jofep Phelps	0—5—0
	William Phelps	0—9—0
	good wife Palmer	0—2–10
	Timothy Palmer	0—2—6
	Humfrey Prior	0—2—6
	John Petybons wife	0—0—6
r	abram Randall	0—2—6
	Thomas Ruly	0—1—3
	James Rifing	0—5—0
	John Rifing	0—1—6
	Hanna Rifing	0—1—3
	famuell Rockwl	0—2—0
S	John ftrong	0–11—0
	return ftrong	0—5—0
	Thomas ftouton	0—2—6
	Hanna fhadock	0—1—3
	Jofep fkinner	0—2—6
	nicolas fenchon	0—2—6
	John faxfton	0—1—3
	gorg fanders	0—1—3
	John Williams wif	0—4—0
	John Kennard	0—2—6
	famuell Wilfon	0—1—3

1 Probably this name should be Thomas Buell.

[93] Aguſt ye . 17 . 1677 .

I here ſet down what children has ben Born in Windſor from our begining hether to ſo fare as I ame able to find out

A	mr Thomas Allyn	8
	Benidictus Aluard	5
	Allixandr Aluard	7
	gorg Allixandr	5
	edward Admes	1
B	John Biſſell snr	1
	John Biſſell iunr	8
	Thomas Biſſell	9
	Samuel Biſſell	6
	Nathanell Biſſell	7
	Thomas Barber snr	6
	Thomas Barber iunr	4
	Samuel Barber	2
	John Barber	2
	Thomas Buckland snr	8
	Timoty Bukland	6
	Nicolas Bukland	3
	Thomas Bukland inr	1
	Richard Birg	5
	Danell Birg	3
	Jeffery Baker	5
	William buell	7
	Samuell buell	1
	Thomas Baſcom	3
	John Bartlet	5
	Beniamn Bartlt	6
D	Thomas Dewey	6
	Thomas Deble	6
	Iſrell Deble	4
	Ebenzr Deble	5
	Samuel Deble	5
	Job Drak	7
	John Drak	11
	Job of John Drak	2
	Henery Denſlo	8
	John Denſlo	9
E	Joſias eleſwort	9
	Begat egelſton	7
	James egelſton	8
	James enno	3
ff	Water ffylar	6
	ſuroball fylar	5
	william fylley	7
	ſamuel fylley	7
	ambros fouler	7
	ſamuel forwrd	2
G	ſamuel grant	8
	mathew Grant	3
	Tahan Grant	6
	John grant	3
	Jonathan gellet snr	7
	Jonathan gelet iunr	3

	Eſay Bartlet	1		cornelus glet	8
	John Brooks	8		Joſep gillet	7
	John Bancroft	5		John gillet	2
	Peter Brown	10		nathan gillet	8
				Thomas gunn	4
C	m^{r} Danell Clark	9		Edward griſold	6
	c Aron Cook	7		gorg griſwold	9
	nathanell cook	7		Joſeph griſwld	3
	m^{r} chancy	2		William gaylar iun^{r}	7
	edward chapman	8		Waltr gaylar	7
	John caffe	6		ſamuel gaylar	6
	Henery curtic	2		John Gaylar	4
	Joſep clark	2		Joſep gaylar	2
	Joſua carter	3			
	ſeborn cotten	1			
	195			227	

[94] G	John Grifen	10	N	Capten Newbery	9
	Jacob Gibbes	7	O	Thomas orton	4
	Samuel Gibbes	7		John owen	11
				Joſias owen	1
H	Thomas Holcom	8		John oſbon sn^{r}	10
	Joſua Holcom	3		Robard ould	2
	nathanel Hokom	2	P	ould m^{r} Phelpes	2
	benaga Holcom	2		ſamuell Phelps	9
	William Haydn	3		Nathanell Pinne	2
	Danell Hayden	4		Nathanell Phelps	4
	John Hofford	8		Timothy Phelps	6
	Nicolas Hayt	4		gorg Phelpes	6
	Robard Hayward	5		Iſack Phelps	3

	John Haks	11
	Joſias Hull	10
	mical Homfrys	7
	luke Hill	7
	Anthony Howkins	3
	John Hodgs	5
	Anthony Hoſkns	9
	Thomas Hoſkins	1
	John Hillar	9
	Timothy Hall	6
	chriſtophar Huntington	1
	arth. Henbery	1
J	gorg Jeffery	3
	William Jeſs	1
K	mark Kelcy	1
L	John Loomys	13
	Joſeph loomys	8
	Thomas loomys	10
	Samuell loomys	5
	Nathanell loomys	10
	John lewes	1
	John lundon	2
M	Deckn moor	3
	John moore	5
	Samuell marſhal	9
	John mawdſly	5
	John moſſes	9
	Edward meſengr	3
	Andrew moore	2
	Thomas maſkell	6
	Abraham Phelps	
	Joſep Phelps	
	John Phelps	
	Joſep of W . Phelps	
	John Portr snr	2
	John Porter nou snr	12
	John Porter iunr	4
	mr Pinne	6
	ſamuel Pinne	2
	Eltwed Pumery	5
	Caleb Pumery	1
	Nicolas Palmer	4
	Timothy Palmer	6
	Samuell Pond	4
	Thomas Parſon snr	8
	Thomas Paſon iunr	3
	John Pettebon	3
	Homfery Prior	2
	Iſack Pond	-
	William Farſon	
	John Petebon	3
R	John Rockwell	7
	ſamuell rockwel	6
	Thomas Ruly	2
	Thomas Rimington	
	ebenezr Farſon	1
S	John ſtrong snr	6
	John ſtrong iunr	4
	Return ſtrong	7

	ſimon milles	6
	235	
[95] S	Richard ſaxſton	6
	Henery ſtilles	5
	John ſtiles	2
	Thomas ſtoughton	7
	John ſhare	1
	mr criſtopar ſandrs	1
T	ſtephn Terey	4
	John Terey	8
	Peter Tilton	3
	ſtephen Taylar	8
	[O]wen Tudor	5
	Thomas Thornton	5
	John Taylar	3
	John Tomſon	2
	willim Trall	2
	Timothy Trall	10
v	richard vore	1
w	mr Henery wolcot	7
	Henery wolcot iunr	6
	ſimon wolcot	7
	mr John warham	4
	Robard winc[hel]	6
	Richard weller	6
	Nathanell winchell	4

177

ſume omited in former records being goon yet had children born her

as capten maſen	4	ye hol ſum
mr Roſeter	6	195
William Rockwell	1	227
Samuell Alyen	6	235
ſimon Hayt	2	177
William Hulbard	2	141
mr ludlo	1	050
nicolas Palmer	4	1025
elias Partman	2	of thes died
Thomas Horten	1	128
mathias ſenchon	3	
frances ſtills	4	
mr william Hill	1	
mr Hueit	1	
Walter Hayt	3	
mathais ſenſhon[1]		
William Hanum	4	
richard ſamways	3	
richard bidwel	1	
John banks	1	
	50	

1 Crossed out.

Jonathan winchell	-
Daued winchell	3
Robard watſon	7
Arter williams	1
Beniamen woodbridg	
John williames	7
John willim iuu^{r}	3
nicolas wilton	2
ſamuell wilſon	2
	141

[96] 1732/3[1]

M^{r} grant book of Cordes
M^{r} grant book

[97] The a count of Parſons taken into church communon and years when . that are now liuing . decm^{r} . 22 . 1677 .

only yet liuing that came from	women from docheſtr
Docheſter in full communion	m^{sts} Phelps .
m^{r} wolcot sn^{r} . m^{r} witchfeld .	Decon moors wif .
m^{r} Pinne . waltr fylar .	ye wido Gillet
mathew Grant . gorg Philups	richrd vors wif
Thomas Deble sn^{r} . Ricrd Vore	ſiſtr fylar . siſtr Deble
Abram Randall .	

---

men taken in here .		women taken in here	
William Phelps . noumbr .	1639 .	mst . Pinne . febary .	1639
John loomys . october .	1640 .	wido Drak . febry .	1639 .

1 The writing on this page is not Matthew Grant's.

Benidicts Aluard . octobr .	1641 .
Robard Haward . July .	1642 .
m^{r} Danell clark . Juen .	1643 .
ſtephen Taylar . march .	1644 .
Robard Watſon . ianury .	1649 .
Water Gaylar . may .	1651 .
capten Newbery . aprel .	1658 .
Jacob Drake . aprel .	1658 .
ſamul Rockwel . aprl .	1662 .
Jonatan gillet . aprel .	1662 .
Peter Brun & nathanl	
cook . both Juen . 22 .	1662
nathanl Loomys . may .	1663
cornels gillet & Timoty	
Bukland both Janury .	1665 .
John gaylar & Thomas	
loomas both . Aprell .	1666 .
John mawdſly . octobr .	1666 .
m^{r} Natl chancy . Janry .	1667 .
ſamul filly . decmbr .	1670 .
ſamul fforwrd . otobr .	1671 .
ſamul Barker . aprel .	1672 .
Timoty Hall . aprel .	1672 .
Nathanl Biſſell ſeptm^{r} .	1673 .
William ffille . march .	1673 .
ſamuel Gaylar . Juen .	1674 .
ſam . fillis wife . decm^{r} .	167[1]

mst . wolcot . aprl .	1640 .
f . gaylrs wif apl .	1645 .
B . alurds wif . ianr .	1647 .
n . fucous . wif . ianry	1649 .
w . fillys wif . iuly .	1651 .
n . coks wif . aguſt .	1652 .
mst nubery . aprl .	1655 .
J . lomas wif aprl	1655 .
Jo . draks wif . apl .	1655 .
cap . clarks . wif . aprl .	1658 .
Jos . lomis . wif . dcm^{r} .	1660 .
ſara gaylar &	
o . Tudors wif . aprl .	1661 .
J . Portrs wif . may .	1663 .
H . dnſlo . wif . aprl .	1665 .
T . allins wif . retrn	
ſtrongs wif . tim . buc	
klands wif . ianury .	1665 .
H . wolcots wif . John	
mors wif . Tho . lomas	
his wif . all aprel .	1666 .
Jac . draks wif . iuen .	1666 .
ſten Tailrs wif . aguſt .	1666 .
J . ſtrongs wif . aguſt .	1666 .
elſwrts wif . & s . gibes	
wif bot ſeptm^{r}	1666 .
ſam . bakrs wif . octo	1670 .
ſam . fillis wif . decm^{r} .	1670 .
mary ſaxſton . aprel .	1671 .

1 This line is crossed out.

nat . wncls wif . aguſt . 1671 .
cor . gilets wif . febr . 1671 .
nat . lomis . wif . ſeptm[r] . 1673 .
elizabt chapman . Aprel . 167[ ]

[98] John Biſsel[1]

[99] he[re] I fet dune ye times of ſacraments admineſtred .
Janury . 16 . 69 . a ſacrament which
ye church had not had . 2 yers . 12 weks .

---

march . 6 . 69 . a ſacramnt . 7 weks ſenc
Juen . 5 . 70 . a ſacramnt . 13 . weks fenc
aguſt . 14 . 70 . a ſacramnt . 10 . weks fenc
octo[r] . 16 . 70 . a ſacramnt . 9 weks ſenc
deſm[r] . 25 . 70 . a ſacrmnt . 10 . weks ſenc
febry . 26 . 70 . a ſacr . 9 . weks fenc
aprel . 23 . 71 . a ſacr . 8 . weks ſenc
Jue[n] 25 . 71 . a ſacr . 9 . weks ſenc
ſeptm[r] . 3 . 71 . a ſacr . 10 . weks ſenc
noum[r] . 5 . 71 . a ſacr[t] . 9 . weks ſenc
Janur . 7 . 71 . a ſacr . 9 weks ſenc
march . 10 . 71 . a ſacr . 9 weks fenc
may . 5 . 72 . a ſacr . 8 weks ſenc
noum[r] . 17 . 72 a ſacr . 28 . weks ſenc
febry . 23 . 72 . a ſacr . 14 . weks ſenc
aprl . 27 . 73 . a ſacr . 9 weks ſenc
iuen . 29 . 73 . a ſacr . 9 weks ſenc
aguſt . 24 . 73 . a ſacr . 8 . weks ſenc

1 Not in Matthew Grants handwriting.

octo^{r} . 9 . 73 . a facr . 11 weks fenc
Janur . 11 . 73 . a facr . 9 weks fene
marc . 15 . 73 . a facr . 9 weks fenc
July . 5 . 74 . a facr . 16 weks fenc
feptm^{r} . 6 . 74 a facr . 9 weks fenc
noum^{r} . 8 . 74 a facr . 9 . weks fenc
July . 25 . 75 . a facr . 28 . weks fenc
octo . 3 . 75 . a facr . 10 . weks fenc
febr . 13 . 75 . a facr . 10 . weks fenc
may . 7 . 76 . a facr . 12 . weks fenc
feptm^{r} . 3 . 76 . a facr . 17 . weks fenc
febry . 18 . 76 . a facr . 24 weks fenc
may . 6 . 77 . a facr . 11 . weks fenc
aguft . 12 . 77 . a facr . 14 weks fenc

---

this was ye laft before D . moor
dyed .

[100] In Decon moors a counts . ye church deter to him for bread from . 15 . Juen . 1666 . to . 11 . Janury . 1673 . for 27 . facramnts

2^{l}—14—0

Du for wine		more for bread	
Aguft . 14 . 70	0—18—0	14 facraments	1—8—0
octob^{r} . 16 . 70	0—13—4		
Decem^{r} . 25 . 70	0—13–10		4—2—0
febry . 26 . 70	0—12—6		
aprel . 23 . 71	0—14—6		
Juen . 25 . 71	0—13—0		

ſeptm^r . 3 . 71	0—15—9
for a caſk of wine	
to ſam . loomis	2— 6—0
noum^r . 17 . 72	0—14—0
febr . 14 . 72	0—11—0
aprl . 27 . 73	0—12—0
Juen . 29 . 73	0—10—6
aguſt . 24 . 73	0—13—1
noum^r . 9 . 73	0—12—6
Janri . 11 . 73	0—11—6
	11-11—6

more after this	
a 11 gallons ½ at	
4^s p galon . is	2^l--6—0
more win	0-12—6
in . 76 . win	0-12—4
in . 76 . win	0-13—0
in . 76 . win	0—8—0
in . 77 . win	0—7—0
agust . 77	0—9—0
a caſk	0—3—6
	5—11-4

[101] [ ] moors acounts
[ ] granted febry . 10 . 73 receiued of ye [
at 2[ ]arſon and by what he granted in 75 . 2[

reſeaued of that leuey and of
former leuies vn paid . 6—4—0

---

of John loomys for both	7^{s}--0
his owne	4—0
Richard vore	4—0
Capten Clark	4—0
georg Phillups	2—0
Jo[hn] ſtrong	2—0
Timothy Buckland	7—0
Nicolas ſenſhon	2—0
Samuell Marſhall	3—6
Benidictus Aluard	4—0
robard watſon	6—0
m^{r} pinne	4—0
Thomas Deble	3—6
Thomas loomas	4—0
Peter Brown	2—0
ſamuell Barker	1—0
mathew Grant	2—0
Walter Gaylar	4—0
Capten n[e]wbery	4—0
Timothy Hall	2—0
Thomas loomas more	3—0
m^{r} forward	2—0
william ffilley	2—0
m^{r} Chancy	2—0
nathanell loomys	4—0
Hanna Drak	2—0
Stephen Taylar	4—0

Abraham Randal	4—0
John ſtrong	2—0
John loomys	4—0
him ſelfe	4—0
m^{r} chancy	2—0
ſamuel Rockwl	2—0
ſamul gaylar	1—6
nathanl loomys	4—0
Thomas loomys	4—0
m^{r} Pinne	4—0
Walter gaylar	4—0
mathew grant	2—0
ſergnt Aluard	4—0
William filley	4—0
John mawdſly	4—0
Jonatan gillet sn^{r}	4—0
Richard Vore	4—0
william Phelps	4—0
mst Phelps	2—0
Nathan gillet	6—0
ſtephen Taylar	4—0
Peter Brown	2—0
leftnant ffylar	4—0
Hanna moore	2-[ ]
Hanna drake	2—0
m^{r} Wolcot	4—0
Jonatan gillet iun^{r}	2—0
capten clark	4—0
ſamuel ffilley	4—0
ſamuel gibbs	1—0

Jonathan gillet iun[r]	2—o	ſamul Bater[1]	5—o
Samuell ffilley	4—o	m[st] Allyn	5—9
John mawdſly	2—o	m[r] Corniſh	4—o
Abraham Randall	4—o		
Cornelus gillet	2—o		5-13—3
m[r] Wolcot	4—o	cornels gillet	o—2-[ ]
ſamuell Rockwell	2—o		
ſamuell gaylar	3—6		
leftenant ffylar	4—o		
wido Buckland	3—o		
Hanna moore	2—o		
ſamuell gibbes	3—o	wth formr	
	6—6—6	12—1—9	

[102 Blank page.]

[103] [ ]
dafter of Nathell biſſell ware maried [ ]

Joſeph ſonn of Joſeph loomas & lidea dafter of John Drake w[ ]
married . Aprell ye . 10 . 1681 .

John ſonn of James enno and mary daughter of ebene
zer deble ware maried by capten Newbery . may ye
tuſday before ye election cort in 1681 . may . ye 10 . day .

Joſua Welles and Hanna Buckland daughter of
Thomas Buckland sner ware maried by capten Newbe[ ]
Auguſt . ye . 11 . 1681 .

1 Probably an error for Samuel Baker.

Thomas fonn of georg grifwold and Hefter daufter o[ ]
Job Drake ware maried by capten Newbery . aguft . 11
1681 he is 23 yere old nixt decmbr . 29 . fhe 19 yer . ye 10 of octo

epram Bancroft and fara daughter of John ftilles ware
maried . may ye fift . 1681 .

[104] nathaniell grant
Wm Grant T: Grant[1]

[105 Blank page.]

[106] [ ] the year 1717 I Set down [all that][1]
[ha]ue dyied in Elenton to the year 1740
left Ellsworth was killed by falling [of a tree]
Isibe penye died
John Burg died
Insine John burah lost a child died
Samuell Gibs lost a daughter died
Samuell pney lost a daughter died
Nathaniell Grant a child died
Gody graymes died
Ephriam Napes wife died
Nathaniell tayloer died
Daniel Eten died
Capt Ellsworth a child dyed
left Hubbord a child dyed
Daniell Eteen a child dyed
Willam Carter too children dyed

1 These names and records are not in Matthew Grant's handwriting.

Stefen paine a child dyed
Symon Chapman dyed
[107] Insine John burah Six children bo[rn]
Samuell Gibs three children bor[n]
Nathaniell taylor three Children
Samuell Gibs Junr to children
Daniell Eten three children
Nathniell Grant to children
Nathaniell Grant Juner three childr[ ]
Benigman Grant too children
Capt Elsworth fife children
Left^{t} Hubbard too Children
Cartee[1] one chid
Simon person on child
Dauid chafen three children
Strickland too children
tim Scot one child
Samuell porson one child
Gidon Skiner on child
too demmans to childrens
Craa one child
three pineys Sefen children
dauies one chld
m^{r} mekinstre too children
booth four children
too drak four children
pers [ ]il[ ]

canad on ch[ ]ld
tomsons three Children
John burah on child

[108 Blank page.]

1 Perhaps an error for Carter.

EARLY

TOWN VOTES

1641 - 1642

The single leaf measuring 7½ by 11½ inches, somewhat frayed on the outer margin, on which the following record is written, was presented to the Connecticut Historical Society, with other manuscripts of an early date, in June 1842 by Sidney Stanley of Tolland. It is evidently from a lost volume containing the record of the earliest orders or votes of the town of Windsor. The orders or votes are in the handwriting of Dr. Bray Rosseter, the town's first recorder, and would appear to have been consecutively numbered from the first; a method followed by the same recorder in making his entries in the Windsor Town's Law Book. Orders numbers 28 to 32 are written on the obverse and numbers 33 to 39 on the reverse page of the leaf. Missing words or letters have been added in brackets.

This leaf was first printed in December 1894; but less than a dozen of the copies then printed were ever distributed.

Tho: ffford hath allowed ſoe much land behind the meade at Podancke wch was ff[or]merly graunted bray Roſſeter & Richard Vore, in
28 liew of the remaynder of meade ꝑmiſed m^{rs} Tilly: to the valew of eleuen pounds, the ground to be valued at one ſhilling ꝑ acre, vntill it amounts vnto the ſumme aforeſd.

Octob. 4th 1641.

Its ordered that noe man ſhall fill any tymber within the lybertyes [of] the plantation for Pypeſtaues or any other vſe intending to fell
29 or ſend them o[r] it out of the towne, wthout ſpēall allowance, eyt[her] from the towne or the ſeuen men, and this order to be in force vn[til] it be appealed.

Its ordered that all cornefeilds ſhallbe in there fences repayre[d and] ſoe maynteyned both winter & ſommer, firmely as it ſhallbe iud[ged] ſuffycient by the ou^{r}viewers of the fence, and if any treſpaſſ come
30 [by] the inſufficiency of the fence, by the ſd fence to be ſatiſfyed. & in caſe the ſd insufficient fence, be not repayred within t[he] warning, ꝑuided it be feaceable, they shall pay one ſhilling ꝑ [day] for eu^{r}y dayes neglect.

Its farther ordered that if any ſwine be found wthin any corne [feild] & pounded, that the ſd hogs ſhall pay eightpence ꝑ hogg [according] to a former order, they ar to be kept in the pound tw[o] dayes [with] warning to the [owner?], and if he [redeam?] them not by
31 compoſ[ition] or paym^{t} in that tyme, the hogs ſhallbe lyable to be ſ[old for] the treſpas, and returning the remaynder to the owner, and i[f] the Hayward neglect any time or wth a[ny] ꝑſon to require leuy, or by compoſition to receiue ſatiſfaction according to the [tenor] of this order the ſd Hayward ſhall pay fiue shillings for eu[ery] ſuch neglect, wch is in the power of eyther of the ſeuen men [to] exact it of him.

Nouemb. 5th 1641.

Its ordered that thoſe men that ar appoynted to view the fences
abo[ut] the cornefeilds they ſhall immediately attend there office
and ch[arge] and in caſe they proue neligent in there office vide^{t}:
to ouerview [the] fences at leaſt once in two m[on]eths, and to
p^{r}ſent at euery towne meeting of the seuen men, wether defectiue
32 or not, they ſhallbe lyab[le] to five ſhillings on euery default, and
in caſe any fence be inſ[uffi]cient after warning, and three dayes
expyred according to the form[er] order, eyther the viewers of the
fence ſhall mend it or cauſe it [to] be mended vnder the foreſd
penalty, and for there ſatisfaction [to be] payd out of the forfeyture
allowed in the order that is concer[ning] the fence:

Its ordered that Robert Winchell & richard Wellar for the northſide
of the Riuulett ſhallbe Hayward[s], and George Phelps for the
ſouthſyde, & they ſhall p^{r}ſently be in office, vppon all occaſions as
33 they ſee fitt they ſhall goe through all the cornefeilds in charge &
pound all hogs they find, and for there pay at 8^{d} ꝑ hogge, they ſhall
receiue eyther in mony or corne at 2^{s} 8^{d} ꝑ buſhell, & the ſd pay
ſhallbe made by the owners of the Swyne eyther p^{r}ſently or ſub-
ſcribe for the certayne paym^{t} thereof before the hoggs be deliu^{d}
out of pound:

ffebruary. 21. 1641.

Its ordered that the way betwixt Henry Styles & James Eggleſtons
there homelotts downe to the greate riuer, ſhallbe allow[ed] for a
publicke highway for horſe & droue to Agawam & the Bay, and
34 from thence to the bridge & ſoe by the head of Plimouth meade
downe to Harteford.

Aprill 4th 1642.

Its ordered that there ſhallbe a highway betwixt m^{r} Witchfeilds, &
m^{r} Marſhalls homelotts, to paſſ from the highway before the little
meade weſt aboue m^{r} Witchfeilds, and then to croſſ the homelotts
northward vntill they fall into the highway that goes vnto the mill,
the common fence of the aforeſd highway to be made & meynteyned
35 wholy by m^{r} Witchfeild, John Moore, Tho; Moore, m^{r} Branker, m^{r}
Nowell Tho: M^{r}shfeild m^{r} Williams & Richard Vore, ꝑuided allſo
that if the aforeſd ꝑſons can agree to allter the ſd way, & ſettle it
betwixt m^{r} Whitings & S[amu]el Allens homelotts wth all thoſe
[ꝑſons] that haue intereſt in the ſame, they haue liberty therevnto.

Its ordered that the gate going into the greate meade, as allſo the
36 gate going into the little meade before m^{r} Warehams ſhallbe kept
ſhutt, & in caſe any leaue them open, they ar to pay 1^{s} for euery
ſuch default, 4^{d} whereof is to be payd to the ꝑſon tha[t shall] dis-
couer the ſame, the reſt to be returned into the tow[ne.]

Its ordered that there ſhall be a pound made on the ſouth of the
37 Riuulett at a puplicke charge & m^{r} Porter & Bray Roſseter to haue
power to p^{r}ſs any to the worke.

Its ordered that noe cattle ſhallbe free to goe in any meades y^{t} ar
planted, on this ſyde of the greate riuer or ouer the greate Riuer
38 from the fifteenth of march to the fifteenth of October, or an[y]
meadowes that ar for graſſ, vnleſſ the ſd Cattle ar kept by a keep[er]
or in cloſed ground in a mans owne ꝑpriety, in caſe any cattle ar
found, or ꝑued wthin the foreſd tyme wthout ſpetiall attendance
according to the tenor of this order they are to pay 8^{d} ꝑ head for
euery ſuch default, all former orders revoked concerning this ꝑticular.

June 3d. 1642.

Mr Hill, Wm Gaylard, Tho: fford, Bray Rosseter, Tho: Thorneton, Henry Woolcott, & John Moore ar chosen to agitate the affayres of
39 the towne fm̄ to the order & power giuen by the Court, for the yeare ensuing. mr Hill is chosen Moderator.

LISTS

OF

FREEMEN

1669, 1703

The two documents here printed were probably among the manuscripts presented to the Society in June 1842 by Sidney Stanley of Tolland.

The earlier of the two is written on both sides of a folio leaf in the hand of Matthew Grant. In addition to the list of Windsor freemen the paper gives the names of those who were, probably in 1669, inhabitants of "mafaco," now Simsbury; lists of Windsor deputies for 1674 and 1676, also a list of persons voted for in the autumn of 1675 for election as assistants the following spring.

The second and later list is written on one side of a folio leaf in an unidentified hand.

Octobr 7th 1669. Acownt taken of all ſuch Parſons as dwell with in the Limets of Windſor, and have bin approued of to be freemen, and alowed to take the oath of freedom.

A mr Allyn: Mathew x
Allyn Thomas
Aluard Benedictus

B Barber John . x
Biſsell John senr x[1]
Biſsell John iunr
Biſsell Thomas
Biſſell Samuell
Biſſell Nathanell
Bartelet John . x
Brown Peter
Bewell William
Buckland Timothy
Buckland Nicolas
Burnam Thomas
Baker Samuell

C mr Chaney Nathanell x[1]
he dos not refuſe: but only for beare ye oth till after ye nixt court .
mr Clark Daniell
Cooke Nathanell
x Chapman: Edward[1]
Coult . John
x Crow Chriſtopher

D Deble Thomas senr
Denslow Henery x[1]
Denſlow John
Drake John
Drake Jobe
Drake Jacob .

E x Egelſton Beagat[1]
Egelſton James x[1]
Egelſton Thomas
Eleſworth Joſiah
x Elmor Edward[1]
Eanno James

F mr ffitch Joseph
ffilly William
ffiſh William x[1]
ffylar Walter
fford Thomas x

G Gaylar William x
Gaylar Walter

1 The "x" is a later entry.

Gaylar Samuell
Gaylar John
x Gillet Jonathan sen^{r}[1]
x Gillet Nathan
Gillet Jonathan iun^{r}
Gillet Cornelus
Gillet Joſeph x
Gibbes Jacob
Gibbes Samuell
Grant Mathew
Grant Samuell
Grant Tahan
Grant John
Griſwold Georg

H Hayden Daniell
Hall Timothy
Hofford John
Hoſkins Anthony
Hayward Robart
Holcom benaga x

L Loomys Joſeph
Loomys John
Loomys Thomas
Loomys Samuell x
Loomys Nathanell

M Marſhall Samuell x[1]
Madeſly John x[1]

x milles Simon[1]
x Moore John sen^{r}[1]
Moore John iun^{r}
Moſes John
Molton William

N m^{r} Newbery Beniamen

O owen John
oſbon John sen^{r}

P x m^{r} Phelps William sen^{r}[1]
Phelps William iun^{r}
Pinne Houmfery
Pinne Nathanell
Phillups Georg
Porter John
Palmer Nicolas
Palmer Timothy
x Phelps Gorg
Phelps Timothy
Pomry Eltwed x
Phelps Jſack x
Phelps Abraham

R Randall Abraham
Rockwell John x
Rockwell Samuell
x Rowly Thomas[1]

1 The "x" is a later entry.

S Senchon Nicolas
Stilles Henery
Stilles John
Stoton Thomas
Strong John
Strong Returne

T Taylar Stephen
Tory John x[1]
Trall William x[1]
Trall Timothy
Tudor owen

V Vore Richard

W mr Warham John x
Watfon Robart
mr Wolcot Henery x[1]
x Wolcot Simon[1]
Wolcot Henry iunr
mr Witchfeld John x[1]
Williams John
Winchell Nathanell
Winchell Jonathan x[1]

---

octobr John wollcot[2]
12.70. Zurrobl fylar
Jofep grifwold
John gaylar iunr
Dauid winchell
Danell Birg
John fylar
John Gillet
Thomas Bukland

Thefe Are Parfons that haue ben of Windsor : But now stated in habitant of mafacò, and this yeare are left out of Windfor lift of eftates yet are owned free men of this Juriousdiction .

Barber Thomas
Cafse John
filly Samuell
griffen John
Houmfey micall
Hill Luke
x mafkell Thomas[1]
Pinne Samuell
Pettebon John
Skiner Jofeph
Holcomb Jofuay
buell Peter
Phelps Jofeph
Ruly Thomas[2]
milles Simon[2]

---

1 The "x" is a later entry.
2 These entries are made in a blue ink.

aprel 28 . 74 . depetis chofen
Decen . moor .
captn Newbry
John lomis for referu

---

may . 4 . 76 Debtys chofen[1]
Decon more & John loomys

[mr[3]] leet gournr a[n] afista[n][1]
[mr Wyl]les [d]bty . a[n] afifta[n]
[mr N]at[n] gold
[mr] Hr . wolcot
[mr] Joh[n] ali[n]
[mr T]alcot
[mr W]l[m] Jones
mr briant
[mr] bifhop
J nafh
cp r Treat
C . T . Tapen
[Maj] E. Pal[m]es
S Sharm̄
J Wadfwrt

[N]ub bla[nk]
crts bla[nk]
[mr M] bla[nk]
[mr] gb bla[nk]
S . tal bl[nk]
T . fch bl[nk]
T f folet[2]
fo fo
fo

1 These entries are made in a blue ink.

2 Apparently the last three entries were not written by Grant.

3 The letters enclosed in brackets in this list are indicated by a kind of shorthand. The list gives the names of the persons who were nominated in Windsor in September 1675 to be voted for the following April for Governor, Deputy Governor and Assistants, or members of the upper house of the General Assembly. They are William Leete, Samuel Wyllys, Nathan Gold, Henry Wolcott, John Allyn, John Talcott, William Jones, Alexander Bryant, James Bishop, John Nash, Capt. Robert Treat, Capt. Thomas Topping, Maj. Edward Palmes, Samuel Sherman, John Wadsworth, Benjamen Newberry, William Curtice, John Mason, Mathew Gilbert, Samuel Talcott, Thomas Fitch.

A list of the free men in Windſo^{r} taken Aprill 27 1703

Captn Mathew Allyn
q^{r} (?) Allex Allyn
Sam^{ll} Allyn
Jerem Alford
Nath^{ll} Biſſell
Thos Biſſell
Nicho^{s} Buckland
Sam$_{ll}$ Barbor
Joſiah Barbor
Deac Sam^{ll} Baker
Jos$_{h}$ Baker
Jno Birge
Thos
Captn Dan^{ll} Clarke
Jno Clarke
Lt Sam$_{ll}$ Croſs
Nath^{ll} Cooke
Jno Cooke
Joſiah Cooke
Tho :
Jno Coult
Joſhp^{h}
Lt Job Drake
Deac Job Drake
Sam Drake
x Jno Denslow[1]
m^{r} Jno Eliot
Joſias Elsworth

Jonath Elsworth
Benj
Jno Egleſtone
James Enno
m^{r} Jno Filer
Zer : Filer
Capt Jos^{ph} Fitch
Sam^{ll} Forward
Sam$_{ll}$ Filly
Serj^{t} Georg Griswold
Dan$_{ll}$ Griswolde
Thos Griswold
Georg Griswold Ju^{r}
Jno Griswold
Benj Griswold
Ens Josp^{h} Griswold
Corn$_{ls}$ Gillet Senr
Eliez Gaylord
Jno Gaylord
Serj^{t} Nath^{ll} Gaylord
Sam^{ll} Grant Sene^{r}
Jacob Gibbs Sene^{r}
Sam^{ll} Gibbs Sene^{r}
Corn$_{ls}$ Gillet June^{r}
Lt Dan$_{ll}$ Heydon
Antho Hoskins Sene^{r}
Antho Hoskins Junr
Jno Hoskins

1 Crossed out.

Sej^{t} Benaj Holcomb
Benaj Holcomb June^{r}
Mark
Serj^{t} Danll Lomas
Timo Lomas
Nath^{ll} Loms
Jos^{p} Lomas
Thos Lomas
Serj^{t} Nath Lomas
Jno Lomas
Dav : Lomas
Jonath Lomas
m^{r} Ath : Mather
m^{r} Samll Mather
m^{r} Jno Moore
Thos Moore
Samll
Thos Marſhall
Eliak Marſhall
Wm Morton
Jno Mansfeild
Andr : Moore
Ens Newbery
Serj^{t} Jno Osborn
Sam^{ll} Osborn
Joſiah Owin Sene^{r}
Joſeph Owin
Sam^{ll} Piny Sene^{r}
Iſaack Pinny
William Phelps Sene^{r}

Capt Timo Phelps
Joſeph Phelps
Willm Phelps June^{r}
Capt Abr Phelps
Abr
Timo Palmer
Samll Rockwell Sene^{r}
Thos Rowly
James Porter
Lt Ret Strong
Ret Strong Junr
Deac Joſ^{h} Skiner
Serj^{t} Henry Stiles
Serj^{t} Timo Trall
Steph Taylor
Jno Taylor
mic Tayntor
Samll Tudor
Henry Wolcot
m^{r} Jno Wolcot
Simon Wolcot
Henry Wolcot
Wm Wolcot
Rodger Wolcot
Ebenez Watſon
Jededia Watſon
Lt Joſhua Willis
Eliez Hill
Sam^{ll} Moore
Abr Phelps

Stephn Lomas
Jno Denslow
Hez Lomas
Samll Strong
Samll Grant Junur
Peter Brown
John Brown
Cornelius Brown
Nathanll Pinney

Thomas Egleſtone
Nathanll Phelps
John Grimes
Thomas Thrall
Wakfild Deeble
Samll Beaman
Danll Biſſell
Joſiah Phelps Senr

CHURCH CONTROVERSY

1669-1679

The two documents which follow were presented to the Society by Sidney Stanley of Tolland, probably in June 1842. Both are of folio size; the earlier is one leaf written on both sides, the later of two connected leaves with the fourth page blank. Both documents are copies and each one is written throughout in the same hand.

Winſor aprill 28 69

Wheras the honored general aſembly, hath apoynted vs whoſe names are vnderwritten to meete at winſor; as by their order 8th octob 68 doth appare; to indeauor an acom̄odation betweene, the chū, and deſenting breathren. we hauing heard, and duly conſidering what is with vs; concering what haue been by each party, preſented to vs acording to the court order. do preſent ſom things, to the conſideration of each party and all ore ani, therin reſpectiuely concerned; which we do find Irreguler and vncomfortable to each other, reſpectively.

firſt in the generall; whereas there was a generall conſent of chū and towne concerning mr cheeuers and mr Eſtabrooks. It apears it was driuen to an Iſhu by the meſſenger imployed by the chū. and ſoe we ſee noe reaſon. why that ſhould be inſiſted one by way of greeuanc ore offenc, although it had beenn better, Iff the ſayd Iſhu had been ſeaſonably made knowne to the whoale congregation. add heareto alſo that after this; both partys were at one as apears by the next pertickuler

2ly one the churches part. firſt conſidering that the members not in full comunion, had been, together with the reſt of the towne, taken into a concurrence with the chū in full com̄union; in ſending to thoſe reuerend elders in the bay for their adviſe: which referrs to mr cheeuers and mr chauncy. Now to exclude all thoſe. putting mr chauncy alone to the vote only of thoſe in full com̄union, and to the diſsatisfaction; of sundri of thoſe in full com̄union. seemes to vs to haue to great a face of rigor and too great a tendancy to deuiſsion and exaſperaſion of mens ſpiritts. Though we dare not vndertake to ſay how farr the fear of a tumultuous mannadgment which is to apt to ariſe when mens ſpiritts are exaſperated. might ocaſion the officer to lead on ſuch a motion; nor doe we medle at preſent with that queſtion; to whom the right ore power of chouſing chū officers doe belong, but ſpeak only con-

cerning the mañer of acting. 1. cor. 16. 14 let all things [be done with charity] phill 4. [5] let your moderation be known to all men
2ly. wheras after this there were at feuerall times indeauors vfed for a concurrency of the towne with the chũ in full comunion; in the caling of mr chauncy: which is yt in the gennerall we doe not blame but aproue yet in the mañadgment thereoff in fom part there feemes to be wanting of that plainenes, that were verry requifit; in a matter of that nature, Inasmuch as all parfons concerned, were not Informed, either of the deputation, of fuch parfons, bye the chũ, in order to fuch an end. ore that their names; were to be taken down in writing. ore of all things; which they were to confent vnto 2. cor. 11.3 lest yor minds fhould be corupted from the fimplicity yt is in X
3ly whereas the honord generall afembly octo. 10. 67; did graunt liberty to the chũ at winfor to fettle mr chauncy, and cal him to office. which notwithftanding when the chũ was proceeding to the ordination of mr chañ to offic The honored Gour and magiftrats faw caufe, to interpofe; and did advife to delay for fom time in that matter. We doe hartyly wifh That that prefident of the churches non atendant to the fayd advife may not by ani be abufed. althoug we medle not with the eclefiafticall counfell. But defire that all dew honor may refpectiuely be giuen by all court magiftrate and counfell. efpefially it is to be giuen by vs who be foe vnable to Judg of the exegentiall reafons reafons ore apearances; Which drew fourth their refpectiue arts. Tit. 3. 1. putting in [m]ind to be fubiect to principallities and powers, to obey magiftrats

one the townes part

ffirftly inasmuch as the order of the generall court octo. 10. 67 giuing liberty to the diffenting party, to procure another minifter; doth plainly

ſhew; that it was the erneſt ſolicitation, of the ſaid diſsenters that preſt them to that act. And after the ſaid liberty graunted, the matter was ſo perfected ſoe farr to efect, without ani more ſollem Indeavors; for the conſeal ore complianc of the chū therevnto: then yet we vnderſtand were vſed; It were much to be deſired that nothing had been don ſhewing ſo much of ſciſm and ſeperation 1. cor. 1. 12. 13 eueri one of you saith I am of paul I of apollo is X deud
2ly Wheras the honrd generll aſembly, mai. 14. 68 had declared that they ſhould not diſaproue of mr Woodbridge his continuanc there as a lecturer and withall that ac̃eptablenes of his liberty to preach onc a fourtnight on the ſaboth; in caſe mr Warhā and the chū condeſended thervnto. That now by vertu of a towne vote, either ani ſhould promote, ore he proceed to preach on the ſaboth though ſoe as it was. yet it seems to be altogether beſide and beyond the liberty, concluded by the generall court; and we are ſorry that ani ſuch ocaſion of diſtaſt and disturbanc of ſpirit, was giuen to the Chū, and the further deviſſion in the plantation
3ly In asmuch as it is a clear caſe; that publique and ſollem days of thāksgiuing doth ſuperced all lecturs as ſuch. yet in that matter of mr woodbridg preaching one the day of thanksgiuing laſt, there be theſe things to be taken notis off. firſt that after that notis giuen of the thanksgiuing to the congregation by the officer of the chū on the ſaboth before. one ſhould imediatly ſtand vp and giue notis of the lecture to begin soe near to the other ſollem ſeruis, this was publique diſorder. 2ly mr woodbridg preaching that day, as circumſtanced, was a ſecond going beyond the liberty graunted to him by the genrl aſembly., and too to Inconſiſtent with the nature of that ſollem ſeruis of that day. eſpeſially that part ſhould withdraw themſelues from aſembling with the chū; on that day thereby ſo much propending to

ſeperation, on that day of harmonie 1 cor 14 let all things be don decently and in order

ſubſcibed by vs

James Fich[1]
Gerſh Bulkle
Sam̄ wakmn
Joſ eliot

Windsor Dec: 25: 1677

It was agreed by ye Reuerend m^r^ Chauncie, and ye com̄ittee of ye elder church of Chriſt in Windſore: and by ye Reuerend m^r^ Woodbridg, & ye com̄ittee of ye congregation wth him, to call a Councell conſiſting of ye elders and meſſengers of ye fiue Churches, of Hartford, farmington, Wethersfield and Midelton, to heare, confider, & determin, all matters of controuertie y^t^ are still depending between ye societies aforeſaid, or between ye first church & any of ye members thereof: And what they ſhall determin & aduiſe to be attended, by one or both parties, or societies, or ye members therof ſhall be by them ſubmitted unto in point of order both in their preſent and future walke.

Hono^ed^ Reuerend & beloued in o^r^ Lord Jeſus.

The deepe fence y^t^ we haue of ye name of God y^t^ is much conſerned in you, and the choiſe com̄andment of Jeſus Christ, & this is of my com̄andment y^t^ you loue one another, together wth y^e^ ſad [ ] ye diſ[u]nion, & deuition according to y^t^ of o^r^ ſaueor a kingdom deuided againſt it ſelfe cannot ſtan[d] but it is brought to doſſolation, we cannot but conceiue it expedient & neceſſary to com̄end this ſollemly as our joint aduice to your ſelfes, according to what is unanimoſely deſired, by ye two congregations yt we ſhold give our Councell as to your preſent & future walke.

1 These names are in the same handwriting as the text of the document.

1 Firſt y^{t} both congregations reunite & walk together in the ſame way of order. And y^{t} this way of order wherin they ſhould meet in their future walk, be the known ſetled walk of ye firſt Church, wch we underſtand to be ye congregationall way of church order according to ye word of God, as it hath bin declared by ye Sinods in 48 & 62 this to be peacably & orderly attended untill better light in an orderly way doth appear. unto ye X.

2 That ye method of this union be y^{t} theſe members of y^{e} ſecond Congregation who ware of ye firſt Congregation return to ther former ſtation therin either in full com̄union or otherwiſe: And y^{t} all ſuch members of y^{e} ſecond congregation wheither formerly of ye first Church or not being ꝑſons of a competenty of knowledg & unblamable Life be alſoe entertained to full comunion wth ye first Church, And in caſe any diſſatisfaction ſhold ariſe in ye church conſerning ye entertainment of any of the ſaid members, y^{t} then ye Reuerend m^{r} Rowlandson & m^{r} Hooker ſhall examin & paſſe their fence upon y^{e} ꝑſon or ꝑſons objected againſt and according to ſuch Judgment they ſhall be accepted: onely we wold be underſtood y^{t} we account not their going off in a day of difficultie to be a ſufficient impediment to theire full com̄union.

3 That m^{r} Chauncie be continued in his office & imployment acting according to ye profeſſed Congregationall principles as aboue expreſſed, And that m^{r} Woodbridg be receiued to com̄union in all ordinances as occaſion is and admitted for a helpe in preaching jointly wth m^{r} Chauncie y^{t} ther may be better knowledg of each others principles, And if ther be not agreement, ye Councell will reſume their ſeſſion ye firſt wensday in Octob^{r} next hauing for y^{t} purpoſe adjorned to y^{t} time (except ſum exigence in ye meane time give occaſion to ye moderators to call them ſooner together wch by ye Counc[ell] they are impowred to doe) when they may give their

advice for a farther and more full ſetlement, And y^{t} in the meane time both ye Reuerend m^{r} Chauncie, & m^{r} Woodbridg be honorably maintained by the whole towne of Windsore collectiuely.

4 We may not omitte the reall neceſsety of a day of ſollemn humiliation to be obſerued y^{t} you doe jointly chaſten y^{r} ſelues befor ye Lord & be deeply aſhamed for whatſoeuer hath bin provoking to ye eyes of his glory & pour out your hearts unto ye Lord y^{t} he wold in great merty pardon all your ſins, effectually heale your ſpirits, & ſettell you in a right way of goſpell union to ye Glory of God & y^{r} owne eternall welfare.

And Laſtly we doe earneſtly councell & adviſe you to forget all former animoſetys with whatſoeuer of muta[ ] offence & irritation hath by ye uncomfortable motions of a day of temptation fallen in amoug you, And laboring conſientioſly & in ye feare of God, ſoe to carry towards & wth one another as may be for the prays of ye God of peace, & your mutuall comfort, & edification in him wch is indeed ye great end of all ordinances: we beſeech you in ye bowels of Chriſt not to forget y^{e} ſin & ſorrow of a day of contention you now for a conſiderable time haue bin laboring vnder: Alaſs for the dishonor reflected upon the name of o^{r} deareſt Lord, & ye prejudice done to the ſoles of men by this meanes: you haue reaſon to know what ye holy ghoſt saith in the 3^{d} of James 16th where inuiing & ſtrife is ther is confuſion & eury euill worke ye experienc ſadly tells you ye certinty of his word therin: the wisdome from aboue is of another nature & tendancie vers 17th the wisdome y^{t} is from aboue is firſt pure then peacable gentell & eaſie to be entreated full of merfy & good fruit wthout partialety & without hipocreſie y^{t} you may be furniſhed wth what is needfull therin for the attainment of ye end deſired it conſerns you earneſtly to make adreſſes to him y^{t} alone can give it: your ſucſeſs wherin as it would greatly adorn the goſpell & redound by many thanksgivings to ye glory of him who is our Lord & yours, ſoe likewise wold it very much conduce to your advantage & comfort in ye enjoyment of his preſſenc whome to poſſes is all in all 2. Cor: 13: 11 finally brethren farewell be ꝑfect be of good comfort, be of one mind, liue in peaſe & ye God of loue and peaſe ſhall be wth you.

John Tallcott, John Allyn, Joſeph Rowlandſon, Samll Hooker, John Whiting, Nathanell Collins, Joſeph Haines, John White, John Wadsworth, Tho: Judde, Nathanel White James Steele, Eliez: Kimberly, Rob: Warner.

Honored Reuerend & dearly beloued in or Lord Jeſus

Vpon a revew of ye aduice formerly giuen you, wth what is preſented from yrſelues in reference to your condicion therupon, in further ꝑſuit of yt great end of ye ſettelment in peace, we haue upon ſeriouse conſideration, wth hearts lifted up to the God of loue to owen & ſucſeed or endeauors, to ye attanment of ye end aimed at & deſired, concluded upon ye ꝑticulars following as aduiſeable therunto.

1 Concerning the entertainment of theſe of ye 2d church into full comunion wth the first mentioned in the 2d head of aduice in theſe words—And yt all ſuch members of ye 2d congregation &c we doe earneſtly adviſe ye ꝑſons conſerned. yt in order to ſuch comunion, they doe wth readineſs, humility, & chearfullneſs, & in the feare of God adreſs themſelues unto mr Chauncie wth Captn Newbery & John Lomas for examination about their fitneſs in point of knowledg, ſubmitting to teſtimonie in point of converſation, And ſoe being by them found fitte to be preſented & admitted to full comunion by ye conſent of the church. And yt ye church doe wth utmoſt regular extent of charety & all christlike tenderneſs & compaſſion receiue them in ye Lord as becometh ſaints.

2 That m^{r} Chauncie be continued in his office & worke of it as formerly, moreouer, y^{t} m^{r} Woodgridg goe on in preaching the word if he ſee cauſe to ye first of aprill next, & y^{t} the church under the guidance of this preſent Councell wth all meete care & ſpeede labour (wth ye concurance of ye towne) to gaine an able Godly Congregationall man in whome (if God will) they may all meete to ſettell among them in ye worke of Christ, and y^{t} being done m^{r} Chauncie to continew or remooue as by the advice of the Councell ſhall be judged moſt conducing to the peace and edification of the whole.

3 That ye Reuerend m^{r} Chauncie & m^{r} Woodbridg during thire abode in their reſpectuve works allotted to them in Windſore be honorably maintained by ye whole towne of Windſo^{r} collectiuely taken. You may be pleaſed alſoe to take notice y^{t} ye moderators are impowred to call ye councell to a reſeſſion as they ſhall ſee cauſe, appointing time & place for ye meeting.

Now honored & beloued, It is matter of no littell murning y^{t} uppon the acco^{t} of the diſquietments raiſed by ye great ſower of diſcord & hitherto (alaſs) to far continued among you, their ſhould be occaſion for us thus to renewe our applications to you. the great aduantag of ſaint becoming unity among ye people of God, you are not unacquainted wth, y^{t} ye Lord of peace himſelfe may crowne these endeauours wth his blessing moulding ye hearts to a mutuall condecenſion to & compliance wth one another in & according to him, y^{t} you may yet experience the abundant returns of his ſoule edefiing preſſenc in his owen ways, y^{t} of you it may be ſaid there ye Lord com̄andeth the bleſſing euen life for euer more. is ye hearts deſire and prayer of your brethren & ſeruants in Christ. John Whiting

Windſo^{r} ye 2^{d} of ye 8th 1678 Nath^{ll} Collins

In ye name & by ye order of ye Councell.

At a Towne meeting Jan: 14: 1678

The Congregation in Windſore being met, did by their voate chooſe ſixe men who are deſired and impowred to conſult, wth ye preſent Honored & Reuerend Councill & any others able to aduiſe to what ꝑſon to make application unto, to procure him to carry on ye worke of ye miniſtry in this place, & ſoe to return ye counſell or aduice given to the congregation to carry it on to effect, to procure the ꝑson to ſettell amongſt us here in Windſore in ye worke of ye miniſtry. The aboue written is voated & the ꝑsons choſen for a comitee are ye worll m^{r} Wolcot, Captn Newbery, Captn Clarke, John Lomis, Jacob Drake, John Biſſell.

Atteſt John Allyn
James Richards

To ye Church & towne of Windſ^{r}

Hartford 21: 11: 78

Brethren & Neighbours, we haue this day met, & conſidered your preſent ſtate & what we formerly aduiſed you unto namely to procure a meet ꝑson able & piouſe whoſe ꝑſwaſion may aduantage him to guide & leade him in ye Congregationall waye: Two ꝑſons haue come under conſideration, both of good teſtimonie for piety and ability, but we haue no certainty (or at leaſt many of us) of y^{e} ꝑſwaſion of either of them as to church walke, what it will be; The ꝑsons are m^{r} Mather and m^{r} Foſter, the former at hand, and we or y^{r}ſelues may readyly come at his Judgmen what it is, wheither he be ſuiteable for you, & ſoe come to a concluſion about him, & if you find noe difficulty in his Judgment in ye forementioned reſpects and can come to a concurrence among yourſelues in him (wch ſimplye conſidered is in our thoughts moſt eligible) we hope will make for your comfort. but if y^{t} cannot be obtained we ſhall take ye firſt

opertunity to make full inquiry of mr Fofter his pſuafion & if yt be found congregationall, and he otherwife meetly qualefied we fhall advife you to procure him & grant or incoragment therin, we haue not to ad farther at preffent .but yt we are ye hartye defirors & indeauorers (according to or meafure) of your peace & edification.
John Talcott, John Allyn, James Richards, Samll Hooker, Nathanll Collins, John White, John Wadsworth, Thomas Judd, Nathanll White, Robert Warner.
This advice is approued by William Leete Gour Samll Willis.

Janry 27: 1678

The congregation in Windfore being mett, to confider ye return of advice yt ye comittee receiued from the Honored Councell, mr Mather being put to voate ther was forty feauen affirmatiue voats & feauenty one Negatiue or Blanks. and mr Fofter being put to voate th[er] was eighty thr[ee affirmati]ue voates and forty fower Negatiue or Blanks.

attеft Danll: Clarke.

At a meeting of the Congregation in Windfore Jan: 27: 78.
The congregation hauing paffed a voate, wherin they declare theire defire, to procure mr Fofter if he be free, & futeably pſwaded & accomplifhed to carry on the worke of Chrift, in ye miniftry heare amongft us. Doe therfor defire the comittie lately chofen to applye to foe many of the Honod & Reverend Gentelmen wth whome they lately advifed as may be com at, & wth all convenient fpeede procure not onely their concurance but affistance in obteining the faid mr Fofter, prouided it appear by fufficient information from fuch Honored and Reuerend Gent: in ye Maffacufets to whom we fhall applie by or meffengers for their teftimonie, of ye faid Mr Fofter, yt he is not only congregationally perfwaded, but otherwife aecom-

plifhed to carry on ye work of Chrift amongft vs. The aboue written voated by ye Congregation attests Danll Clarke

At a Towne meeting in Windfore Febry 18 1678

There being objection refpecting a voate, about ye comittie, formerly chofen, by the Towne, whether they fhould remaine in ftate, & make further application to the Councell: the Moderator propounded it to ye congregation f[or a] further clearing of ye voate, & defired thefe y^t wa[s] for ye comittee [to]c[onti]n[ue] in [the]ir work[e] to goe to ye fouth fide in y^e meeting houfe y^e others to goe [to] y[^e] No[rth] [si]de, An[d] ther went to y^e fouth fide forty eight, & y^e reft prefently went forth of the houfe & but two remained of y^eNorth fide.

RATABLE LIST

OF

PERSONS AND ESTATES

1686

This document was probably presented by Sidney Stanley of Tolland, possibly in June 1842. The list is entered in a long narrow book consisting, including the cover sheet, of sixteen pages measuring four by twelve and three-fourths inches. It is written in a bold, unidentified hand, different from any of the signatures which appear at the end.

Windſor
Liſt of perſons & Eſtate Rateable
according to Law
1686

Lt Thos Allyn

3 Perſons	54	00
houſe land 6 acs ½	08	00
In plimoth mead: 40 acs	93	00
In Hartford ſwampe 14 acs	14	00
To his part in ye mill	17	00
4 horses: 1 of 1 y	17	00
2 oxen 3 cows 1 of 3 y	25	00
2 of 2 y: 3 of 1 y 6 ſwine	13	00
2 horſes of his ſone	26	00[1]
	241	00

Matthew Allyn

One pſone	18	00
houſe land 4 acs	05	00
in greate meadw 12 acs	25	00
To his pt in mr Warhams houſe land & 1 ac mead	09	00
2 horſes: 2 oxen 1 ſwine	19	00
	76	00

Jeremia Alford

One pſone	18	00
houſe land 4 acs	04	00
vpl: 8 acs	08	00

1 This line is crossed out.

meadow 2 acs	03	16
2 cows: 1 of 2 y: 3 ſwine	13	00
	46	16

Joſia Alford

One pſone 1 Cow	22	00

Thos Allyn Junir

1 pſone 2 horſes	26	00

Cornt John Biſſell

3 pſons	54	00
houſe land 8 acs	08	00
Meadow 6 acs	13	00
Eaſt River mead 19 acs	38	00
2 oxen 4 cows	26	00
5 of 2 y: 2 of 1 y 2 horſes	25	00
1 of 3 y: 1 of 1 y: 4 ſwine	08	00
	172	00

qr Thos Biſſell

5 pſons	90	00
houſe land east ye River 4 acs	04	00
houſe l: weſt ye River 5 acs	05	00
meadow 22 acs	50	00
vpl: 27 acs	26	00
4 horſes: 1 of 2 y: 2 of 1 y	20	00
2 oxen 6 cows 2 of 1 y	38	00
2 of 3 y: 1 of 2 y: 1 of 1 y		
6 ſwine	15	00
	248	00

Samll Biſſell

3 ꝑſons	54	00
vpland 20 acs	18	00
meadow 18 acs ½	38	00
3 horſes: 2 oxen 4 cows		
1 of 3 y: 6 ſwine	47	00
2 of 3 y: 3 of 1 y 1 oxe	14	00
	171	00

Thos Biſſell Junir

One ꝑſone	18	00
meadow 8 acs	18	00
1 horſe of 3 y	03	00
4 cows: 1 of 3 y: 1 of 2 y	21	00
1 of 1 y: 2 ſwine	03	00
	63	00

Nathanll Biſſell

2 ꝑſons	36	00
vpland 31 acres	28	00
meadow 26 acres	57	00
at podunk 10 acs	19	00
vpl: 5 acs	04	00
houſe land 3 acs yt was Lords (?)	03	00
2 horſes 2 of 3 y: 2 of 2 y	18	00
4 oxen: 7 cows 1 of 3 y	51	00
2 of 2 y: 1 of 1 y: 5 ſwine	10	00
	226	00

Timothy Buckland

2 ꝑsons	36	00
houſe land 2 acs ¼	03	00
houſe land 3 acs yt was J Dibles	03	00
In greate mead 10: acs	22	00
In pine mead 11 acs	20	00
2 oxen: 2 cows: 1 of 3 y	21	00
3 of 1 y: 2 horſes: 1 of 3 y		
2 ſwine	16	00
	121	00

Nichos Buckland

2 ꝑsons	36	00
houſe land 7 acs ¼	08	00
meadow 31 acs	69	00
2 oxen: 3 cows: 1 of 3 y	25	00
1 of 2 y: 2 of 1 y 3 horſes	16	00
1 of 3 y: 1 of 2 y: 1 of 1 y		
6 ſwine	12	00
	166	00

Peter Browne

3 ꝑsons	54	00
houſe land 6 acs	06	00
ſwamp 3 acs	03	00
mead 5 acs	09	10
vpl 2 acs	01	10
2 horſes 2 oxen 3 cows	30	00
1 of 2 y: 2 of 1 y: 5 ſwine		
1 of 3 y	12	00
	116	00

Wm Bewels Estate		
houſe land 5 acs	05	00
mead 2 acs ¾	05	04
	10	04
Bartho: Bernod		
12 acs mead	25	00
Samll Barbor		
2 ꝑſone	36	00
house land 7 acs	07	00
vpland 10 acs	09	00
mead 1 ac	02	00
3 horſes: 1 of 2 y 4 oxen	34	00
3 cows 2 of 1 y 6 ſwine	20	00
	108	00
Joſia Barbor		
2 ꝑſone	36	00
vpl: 8 acs	08	00
2 horſes 2 oxen 3 cows		
2 of 2 y 5 ſwine	39	00
	83	00
Samll Baker		
1 ꝑſone	18	00
vpl: 11 acs	10	00
meadow 3 acs	06	00
1 horſe 2 oxen: 3 cows	26	00
1 of 2 y: 2 of 1 y: 3 ſwine	07	00
	67	00

Joſeph Baker

1 pſone	18	00
vpland 8 acs	08	00
mead 1½ acs	03	00
1 horſe: 1 of 3 y 2 cows		
2 of 2 y: 2 ſwine	21	00
	50	00

Danll Birge

1 perſone	18	00
houſe land 5 acs	05	00
vpl: 4 acs	03	00
meadow 8 acs	17	00
1 horſe 2 oxen 2 of 3 y	20	00
2 cows 1 of 1 y 4 ſwine	13	00
	76	00

John Birge

1 perſone	18	00
houſe land 2 acs	02	06
mead 13 acs	29	14
2 oxen 2 cows 1 of 3 y	21	00
1 horſe: 1 of 1 y: 4 ſwine	09	00
	80	00

Joſeph Birg

1 perſon	18	00

Thos Burnum Senir

1 pfons	18	00[1]

1 First written 2 pfons 36.

houſe land & meadow	50	00
2 horſes: 2 oxen: 2 cows	26	00
1 of 3 y: 2 of 1 y: 4 ſwine	09	00
	103	00
Thos Burnum Junir		
2 ꝑſons	36	00
5 acs ½ mead	11	00
1 horſe 2 oxen: 2 cows		
1 of 2 y 2 of 1 y 1 ſwine	27	00
	74	00
John Burnum		
1 ꝑſone 1 horſe 2 oxen		
1 cow 1 ſwine	37	00
Samll Burnum		
1 ꝑſone: 1 hors: 1 cow	26	00
Ephr̄ Bancroft		
1 ꝑſone 1 cow 1 of 1 y	23	00
Samll Burre		
4 acs vpl	04	00
Captn Danll Clarke		
1 ꝑſone	18	00
houſe land 8 acs	09	00
meadw 16 acs	36	00
vpl: 4 acs	03	00

2 horſes 2 oxen 4 cows		
2 of 1 y	36	00
	102	00
Joſia Clarke		
1 pſone	18	00
4 acs vpl:	04	00
1 oxe: 2 of 3 yr 2 cows	19	00
	39	00
1 of 2 y: 2 of 1 y: 5 ſwine	09	00
	48	00
John Clarke		
1 pſone 1 oxe 1 horſe	27	00
Samll Clarke		
1 pſone	18	00
Samll Croſs		
2 pſons	36	00
houſe land 8 acs	08	00
meadow 25 acs ½	57	00
Eaſt ye River 13 acs	13	00
4 acs paſture	04	00
upl: 1 ac: mead 10 acs yt was Higlys	22	00
3 horſes: 2 of 1 yr: 2 oxen	24	00
5 cows: 2 of 2 y: 3 ſwine	27	00
	191	00

John Crofs		
1 ꝑfone	18	00
2 oxen: 2 of 3 y	16	00
	34	00
Henry Chapman		
1 ꝑfone	18	00
Nathll Cooke		
1 ꝑfone	18	00
houfe land 5 acs	05	00
mead 7 acs	14	00
1 horfe 2 cows 2 of 2 y		
1 of 1 y: 1 fwine	18	00
	55	00
John Cooke		
1 ꝑfone 1 horfe	22	00
Thos Cooke		
2 ꝑfons	36	00
house land 5 acs	06	00
mead 15 acs yt was mr Howels	33	00
1 horfe: 4 ccws 2 of 2 y		
1 of 3 y 4 fwine	31	00
	106	00
John Coult		
3 ꝑfons	54	00
vpl: 4 acs	04	00
2 horfes 2 oxen 5 cows	38	00

1 of 3 y: 2 of 2 y 4 ſwine	11	00
	107	00
Dan[ll] Cum̄in		
1 pſone	18	10
John Drake Seni[r]		
1 pſone	18	00
house land 4 ac[s]	04	00
meadow 8 ac[s] ½	16	00
Eaſt y[e] River 10 ac[s]	15	10
4 cows: 1 of 1 y	17	00
	70	10
Job Drake Sone of Jn[o]		
1 pſone	18	00
houſe land 4 ac[s]	04	00
Eaſt y[e] river 12 ac[s]	15	00
1 horſe 2 oxen: 3 cows		
1 of 2 y: 1 of 1 y	29	00
	66	00
Enoch Drake		
1 pſone 1 ac ½ houſe land	19	10
1 horſe 1 Cow	08	00
1 horſe of 2 y	2	
	29	10
Simon Drake		
1 pſone 1 horſe	22	00

Job Drake Senir

1 ꝑſone	18	00
houſe land 19 acs ¾	22	00
In great mead 20 acs	44	00
In litle mead 2 acs ½	05	00
Incloſed land 4 acs	03	00
2 oxen 5 cows 2 of 2 y		
1 of 1 y: 3 horses	52	00
	144	00

Job Drake ſone of Job

1 ꝑſone	18	00
house land 1 acre ¼	01	10
East ye river mead 20 acs	44	00
2 horſes 2 oxen 4 cows	34	00
1 of 2 y: 1 of 1 y: 2 ſwine	05	00
	102	10

Sergt Jacob Drake

1 ꝑſone	18	00
houſe land 11 acs ½	12	00
meadow 14 acs	32	00
In greate meadow 5 acs ½	12	00
East ye River mead 10 acs	24	00
4 oxen: 4 cows: 3 of 3 y	45	00
4 horſes: 1 of 2 y: 5 ſwine	23	00
	166	00

Thos Dible Senir

1 ꝑſone	18	00
houſe land 4 acs	04	10

meadow 5 ac^{s}	10	00
2 cows 1 ſwine	09	00
	41	10
Sam^{ll} Dible		
1 ꝑſone 1 cow	22	00
Thos Dible Juni^{r}		
1 ꝑſone	18	00
Jeremia Dickins		
1 ꝑſone: meadow 2 ac^{s} ½	23	00
1 horſe 1 cow 1 ſwine	09	00
	32	00
John Denslow Juni^{r}		
1 ꝑſone: 4 ac^{s} houſe l: 4^{l}	22	00
Joſeph Denslow		
1 ꝑſone	18	00
Sam^{ll} Denslow		
1 ꝑſone	18	00
vpl: 7 ac^{s}	07	00
meadow 6 ac^{s}	12	00
2 of 4 y: 1 Cow: 1 of 2 y 1 of 1 y: 1 horse 2 ſwine	21	00
	58	00
Serg^{t} Joſia Elsworth		
3 ꝑſons	54	00

houſe land 9 ac[s]	10	00
In greate meadow 6 ac[s]	14	08
Eaſt y[e] River 20 ac[s]	39	12
2 oxen: 5 cows: 1 of 3 y	33	00
1 of 4 y: 2 horſes	09	00
	160	

Joſia Elsworth Junir

1 pſone	18	00
meadow 6 ac[s]	12	00
1 oxe: 2 cows: 1 of 3 y	16	00
1 of 1 y 1 horſe: 1 of 1 y: 1 ſwine	07	00
	53	00

Thos Egleſtone Senir

1 pſone	18	00
house land ½ an ac	00	12
Eaſt y[e] River mead 1 ac ¼	02	08
vpl: 2 ac[s]	02	00
1 cow	04	00
	27	00

Benj: Egleſtone

2 pſones	36	00
meadow 11 ac[s]	21	00
vpl: 2 ac[s]	02	00
2 oxen: 2 cows: 1 of 3 y	21	00
1 horſe 1 of 3 y 1 ſwine	08	00
	88	00

John Eglestone[1]		
1 pſone	18	00
house land 4 acs ½	04	10
1 cow 1 of 1 y	05	00
	27	10

Thos Eglestone Junir		
1 pſone	18	00
house land 4 acs ½	05	00
1 cow: 2 ſwine	06	00
	29	00

John Elmor		
1 pſone	18	00
mead 19 acs	45	00
vpl: 6 acs	05	00
1 horſe 2 oxen: 2 cows	22	00
2 of 3 y 1 of 1 y: 7 ſwine	14	00
	104	00

Edward Elmor		
1 pſone	18	00
meadow 14 acs	32	00
vpl: 6 acs	05	00
3 horſes 1 of 1 y 2 oxen	23	00
2 cows: 1 of 1 y: 6 ſwine	15	00
	93	00

Thos Long mead 4 acs ½	10	00

1 Junir crossed out.

James Enno

1 ꝑſone	18	00
houſe land 12 ac^s	12	00
meadow 4 ac^s	08	00
2 cows 4 ſwine	12	00
	50	00

John Enno

1 ꝑſone 1 cow 1 of 2 y 1 of 1 y	25	00

M^r Joſeph Fitch

2 ꝑſons	36	00
meadow 35 ac^s	84	00
vpl: 11 ac^s	11	00
2 horſes: 2 oxen: 3 cows	30	00
1 of 2 y: 2 of 1 y 2 ſwine	06	00
	167	00

John Filer

1 ꝑſone	18	00
houſe land 11 ac^s	13	00
mead: 18 ac^s ½	39	00
houſe land y^t was his fathers 10 ac^s	12	00
meadow 10 ac^s	24	00
1 horſe 1 of 2 y: 1 of 1 y	07	00
2 oxen 4 cows: 2 of 3 y 2 of 2 y: 1 ſteer 4 y: 3 ſwine	43	00
	156	00

Zerubabell Filer

2 ꝑſone	36	00
vpl: 2 ac^{s} meadow 4 ac^{s}	12	00
2 oxen: 3 cows: 1 of 1 y		
2 horſes: 4 ſwine	35	00
	83	00

Wm Filly

2 ꝑſones	36	00
houſe land 6 ac^{s}: vpl: 12 ac^{s}	18	00
vpl: 6 ac^{s}	06	00
1 hors of 3 y: 2 oxen 2 cows		
1 of 3 y: 2 ſwine	26	00
	86	00

Sam^{ll} Filly

1 ꝑſone	18	00
houſe land 2 ac^{s}	02	00
vpl: 6 ac^{s}	05	00
at greenfeild 5 ac^{s}	04	00
meadow 5 ac^{s} ¾	12	00
vpl: 9 ac^{s}	07	00
1 horſe 1 of 2 y: 2 oxen		
3 cows 1 of 2 y 1 of 1 y	31	00
	79	00

Sam^{ll} Farmoth[1]

1 ꝑſone	18	00
houſe land 3 ac^{s}	03	10
meadow 4 ac^{s} ¾	11	00
1 Cow	04	00
	36	10

1 Samuel Farnsworth.

Ephr̄ French		
1 ꝑſone	18	00
Sergt Georg Griswald		
3 ꝑſons	54	00
vpl: 6 acs ½	06	00
mead 24 acs	46	00
In greate meadow 4 acs	08	00
2 horſes 2 oxen 3 cows	30	00
2 of 2 y: 2 of 1 y: 9 ſwine	15	00
	159	00
Danll Griswald		
1 ꝑſone	18	00
vpl: 3 acs	02	10
mead 9 acs	17	00
1 hors: 1 oxe 3 cows		
1 ſwine 2 of 1 y	24	00
	61	10
Thos Griswald		
1 ꝑſone	18	00
vpl: 2 acs	02	00
mead at Pequanack 4 acs	08	00
1 hors 1 oxe 3 cows 1 ſwine	22	00
	50	00
Sergt Joſeph Griswald		
1 ꝑſone	18	00
vpl: 11 acs	10	00
mead 24 acs	46	00

houſe land y^t was S: Gaylords 4 ac^s	04	00
4 ac^s mead of Sam^{ll} Phelps	08	00
2 horſes 1 of 3 y: 2 of 1 y	13	00
2 oxen 4 cows 1 of 3 y 3 of 2 y: 2 of 1 y 5 ſwine	42	00
	141	00

Joſeph Garret

meadow 4 ac^s ½	10	00

Nathan Gillet $Seni^r$

1 ꝑſone	18	00

Nathan Gillet $Juni^r$

1 ꝑſone	18	00
1 horse	04	00
	22	00

Jonathan Gillet

	18	00
2 ꝑſone	18	00
houſe land 4 ac^s	04	00
meadow 1 ac ½ y^t was S: Gibbs	03	00
meadow 4 ac^s y^t was J Mansfeilds	08	00
2 oxen 2 cows 1 of 3 y 1 of 1 y 1 ſwine	23	00
	74	00

Cornelius Gillet

2 ꝑſons	36	00

house land 8 ac^s	08	00
4 cows: 1 of 2 y 1 of 1 y		
1 ſwine	20	00
	64	00

Joſia Gillet

1 pſone	18	00
vpl: 8 ac^s	07	00
meadow 12 ac^s	24	06
vpl: 6 ac^s	04	10
4 ac^s vpl	04	00
2 horſes 2 oxen 2 cows		
2 of 1 y: 7 ſwine	35	00
	92	06

Jeremia Gillet

1 pſone	18	00
houſe land 5 ac^s	05	00
	23	00

Jno Gillets Estate

vpl: 3 ac^s	03	15

Walter Gaylord

1 pſon	18	00
houſe land 2 ac^s ½	03	00
meadow 13 ac^s	25	00
2 oxen: 2 cows: 1 of 3 y		
1 horſe of 3 y: 2 ſwine	26	00
	72	00

Sergt John Gaylord		
2 ꝑsons	36	00
house land 6 acs	06	00
In greate meadow 8 acs ½	20	08
East ye River 15 acs mead	34	00
2 oxen: 2 cows: 1 of 3 y	21	00
1 of 1 y: 2 horses: 6 swine	15	00
	132	08

Samll Gaylord Senir		
house land 2 acs	2	10
In greate meadow 6 acs ½	14	00
	16	10

Samll Gaylord Junir		
1 ꝑsone	18	00
East ye river 11 acs mead	24	00
	42	00

John Gaylord Junir		
1 ꝑsone	18	00
house land 2 acs	02	05
mead 1 ac ½	03	12
East ye river mead 30 acs	60	00
2 cows: 1 of 2 y: 1 of 1 y		
2 horses 1 swine	20	00
	103	17

Nathll Gaylord		
1 ꝑsone	18	00
vpl 1 ac	01	00
In pine mead 15 acs	27	00

meadw yt was Sergt Drakes 2 acs	04	00
2 oxen 4 cows: 1 of 3 y	29	00
1 of 2 y: 1 of 1 y: 1 horſe		
5 ſwine	12	00
	91	00

Samll Grant Senir

3 ꝑſons	54	00
vpl: & boggs 20 acs	20	00
meadow 3 acs	07	00
2 horſes: 1 of 3 y: 1 of 2 y	13	00
2 oxen: 4 cows: 1 of 2 y		
3 of 1 y: 4 ſwine	35	00
	129	00

Tahan Grant

2 ꝑſons	36	00
houſe land 14 acs	16	00
in greate mead 10 acs ½	24	00
East ye river vpl: 15 acs	15	00
meadow 4 acs	08	00
4 cows: 1 of 1 y: 1 horſe		
1 of 2 y 3 ſwine	26	00
	125	00

Samll Grant Junir

1 ꝑſone 1 hors 1 cow		
1 of 1 y: 2 ſwine	29	00

Widw Mary Grant

houſe land 1 ac	01	00
meadow 10 acs	19	00

In marſh 11 ac^{s}	12	00
2 oxen: 2 cows 1 of 3 y	21	00
1 of 2 y: 2 of 1 y		
3 horſes: 1 of 1 y 2 ſwine	19	00
	72	00

Jacob Gibbs

2 pſons	36	00
houſe land 6 ac^{s}	07	00
mead 10 ac^{s}	23	00
2 oxen: 2 cows 2 of 2 y		
1 horſe 2 ſwine	28	00
	94	00

Sam^{ll} Gibbs

1 pſone	18	00
houſe land 4 ac^{s} ½	06	00
mead^{w} 3 ac^{s} ¾	08	00
vpl & mead y^{t} was Rockwels	14	00
2 oxen 3 cows: 2 of 2 y	26	00
2 of 1 y: 1 horſe 5 ſwine	11	00
	83	00

Ephr̄: Howart

1 ac houſe land	01	00
1 pſone	18	00
meadow 2 ac^{s} ½	05	00
2 horſes: 2 cows 1 of 1 y		
6 ſwine	23	00
	47	00

Danll Heydon

2 pfons	36	00
houfe land 10 acs ½	12	00
meadw 28 acs	60	00
marfh 7 acs	07	00
2 oxen: 4 cows: 1 of 3 y	29	00
4 of 2 y: 4 of 1 y 5 horfes		
2 of 3 y 2 of 2 y: 2 of 1 y:		
8 fwine	52	00
	196	00

Widw Hosford

1 pfone	18	00
houfe land 19 acs ¼	19	10
meadow 16 acs	35	00
fwamp l: 6 acs	05	10
1 horfe 5 cowes: 6 fwine	31	00
	108	00

Willm Hofford

1 pfone	18	00
at Hoyts meadow 9 acs of mrs Hoyt	18	00
houfe land 2 acs	02	00
In greate meadow 7 acs	15	00
2 oxen 1 horfe: 1 of 2 y: 1 of 1 y	17	00
	70	00

John Hosford

1 pfone	18	00
fwamp land 4 acs	03	10
4 acs meadow	08	10

2 acs houſe land	02	00
1 horſe	04	00
	36	00

Timothy Hosford

1 pſone	18	00
meadw 4 acs	08	10
1 ac: ¾ houſeland	01	15
4 acs ſwamp land	03	10
	31	15

Anthony Hoskins

4 pſons	72	00
houſe land 14 acs	16	00
East ye river mead 15 acs	30	00
In great & litle mead 9 acs	19	00
1 horſe: 4 oxen 4 cows	40	00
2 of 3 y: 1 of 2 y: 11 ſwine	19	00
	196	00

John Hoskins

1 pſone	18	00
houſe land 4 acs	04	10
meadow 17 ac ½	41	10
pine meadow 13 acs	24	00
2 oxen: 3 cows: 1 of 1 y		
2 horſes 4 ſwine	35	00
	123	00

Mr Joseph Hawlye

houfe land 2 acs ½	02	10
mead 10 acs	22	10
	25	00

John Higly

houfeland 1 ac ½	01	10
m Griswalds mead 12 acs	28	10
	30	00

Benaj: Holcomb

2 pfons	36	00
vpl: 4 acs mead: 9 acs	21	00
1 hors 1 of 3 y 2 oxen	17	00
2 cows 1 of 3: 1 of 2 y		
1 of 1y 1 fwine	15	00
	89	00

Nathll Holcomb

vpl 3 acs	03	00

Sergt James Hellyar

1 pfone	18	00
houfe land 5 acs	05	00
2 cows: 1 of 2 y: 1 of 1 y		
1 fwine	12	00
	35	00

Georg Hays

1 pfone	18	00

1 cow 1 of 1 y: 1 horſe		
1 of 1 y	10	00
	28	00
Mark Kelſie		
2 pſones	36	00
mead: 4 acs vpl: 13 acs	21	00
2 oxen: 3 cows 1 of 3 y		
3 of 1 y: 2 horſes 4 ſwine	40	00
	97	00
John Lomas Senir		
3 pſons	54	00
houſe land 7 acs	08	00
mead 14 acs	33	00
woodl: 4 acs	02	00
Eaſt ye River 16 acs mead	36	00
2 horſes 2 oxen, 4 cows	34	00
1 of 2 y: 4 of 1 y: 4 ſwine	10	00
	177	00
John Lomas Sone of Jno		
2 pſone	18	00
3 cowes: 1 horſe	16	00
	34	00
Joſeph Lomas Sone of Jno		
1 pſone	18	00
4 cows: 1 of 2 y 2 horſes		
1 of 1 y: 5 ſwine	32	00
	50	00

Dan^{ll} Lomas		
1 ꝑſone	18	00
1 horſe 3 cows 1 of 2 y		
4 ſwine	22	00
	40	00

Joſeph Lomas Seni^{r}		
1 ꝑſone	18	00
houſe l: 1 ac	01	05
vpl: 7 ac^{s}	05	00
Eaſt river mead 14 ac^{s}	29	15
3 cows 2 of 2 y: 2 of 1 y		
2 horſes 3 ſwine	29	00
	83	00

Joſeph Lomas Sone of Joſ^{h}		
1 ꝑſone	18	00
vpland 1 ac ½	01	10
2 horſes 2 oxen 3 cows		
1 of 2 y: 2 of 1 y 2 ſwine	36	00
	55	10

Jno Lomas Sone of Joſeph		
1 ꝑſone 1 cow 1 of 1 yr		
2 ſwine	25	00

Thos Lomas Seni^{r}		
1 ꝑſone	18	00
vpland 6 ac^{s}	07	00
meadow 20 ac^{s}	40	00

1 horſe 1 of 1 y: 4 cows		
1 of 2 y: 1 of 1 y 3 ſwine	27	00
	92	00

Thos Lomas Juni^{r}

1 ꝑſone	18	00
m^{r} Clarks land 6 ac^{s} mead	12	00
5 ac^{s} upl 1 ac vpl	06	00
2 oxen 2 cows 1 of 2 y		
3 ſwine	23	00
	59	00

Nathan^{ll} Lomas Seni^{r}

3 ꝑſones	54	00
houſe land 5 ac^{s}	06	10
meadow 6 ac^{s} ½	14	00
at dearefeild 8 ac^{s}	08	00
East ye River 15 ac^{s} mead	35	00
7 cows: 2 horſes: 1 of 1 y		
4 ſwine	41	00
	158	10

Nath^{ll} Lomas Juni^{r}

1 ꝑſon	18	00
2 ac^{s} upl:	02	00
mead 6 ac^{s}	14	00
1 horſe: 2 oxen: 3 cows		
1 of 2 y: 1 of 1 y: 5 ſwine	34	00
	68	00

Josia Lomas

1 pſone	18	00
1 cow: 1 of 1 y	05	00
	23	00

John Lewis

1 pſone	18	00

mr Samll Mather

houſeland 10 acs	11	00
meadow 10 acs	22	00
	33	00
1 horſe: 1 of 3 y: 1 of 1 y		
1 heifer of 3 y: 2 of 2 y	15	00
	48	00

Atherton Mather

1 pſone	18	00
houſe land 4 acs	04	00
1 horſe	04	00
	26	00

John More

4 pſons	72	00
houſe land 8 acs	09	00
In great meadow 8 acs	16	00
In litle mead 8 acs	16	00
In plimoth mead 11 acs	24	00
at dearefeild 11 acs	11	00
Eaſt ye River 3 acs ½	07	00

11 acs mead yt was mr Warhams	24	00
2 horſes 1 of 3 y: 1 of 2 y	13	00
2 oxen: 5 cows: 1 ſwine		
1 of 2 y	39	00
	231	00

Lt Jno Maudsly

house land 3 acs	03	00
meadow 4 acs ¼	10	00
	13	00

Andrew More

1 pſone	18	00
vpland 6 acs	05	00
1 horſe 1 of 1 y: 1 oxe		
2 cows: 1 of 1 y	19	00
	42	00

Wm Morton

1 pſone	18	00
1 cow: 1 of 3 y	07	00
	25	00

John Mansfeild

1 pſone	18	00
houſe l: 14 acs	15	00
meadw 8 acs	16	00
1 hors: 1 of 1 y: 3 cows		
2 of 1 y: 4 ſwine	23	00
	72	00

Capt Marſhalls Estate		
house land 1 ac	01	00
mead: 15 acs ½	33	00
at Hoyts mead 4 acs	04	00
paſture 4 acs	08	00[1]
	38	00

David Marſhall		
1 pſone	18	00
houſe land 5 acs	06	00
at Hoits mead 4 acs	04	00
	28	00

Thos Marſhall		
1 pſone 1 of 3 y	21	00
mead 4 acs ½	10	00
	31	00

Peter Mills		
2 pſons	36	00
vpland at greenfeild 18 acs	18	00
2 cows: 2 horſes: 1 of 1 y		
5 ſwine	22	00
	76	00

Nathan Meſſenger		
1 pſone	18	00
vpl: at greenfeild 10 acs	10	00
1 of 1 y 2 cows: 1 ſwine	10	00
	38	00

1 This line crossed out.

Widow Mofefs

1 pfone	18	00
houfeland 21 acs	21	00
meadow 6 acs	13	00
vpl: 5 acs	04	00
1 hors of 3 y: 3 cows 1 fwine	16	00
	72	00

John Matson

1 pfone 2 horfes	26	00

Capt: Benj: Newbery

1 pfone	18	00
houfeland 4 acs ¾ vpl: 5 acs	10	00
meadow 24 acs	54	00
1 horfe 1 of 1 y: 2 oxen	15	00
5 cows 1 of 2 y 2 of 1 y 1 fwine	25	00
	122	00

Thos Newbery

1 pfone	18	00
Eaft ye River 18 acs mead	40	00
land yt was M Hs	08	00
2 oxen: 2 cows: 1 of 3 y 1 of 1 y: 1 fwine	23	00
	89	00

John Osborn Senir

2 pfons	36	00
houfe land 2 acs	02	10

meadow 14 acs	28	00
vpl: 5 acs	05	00
3 cows: 2 of 3 y: 1 of 2 y		
1 horfe 2 fwine	26	00
	97	10

Jno Osborn Junir

1 pfone	18	00
mead 21 acs	40	00
mead yt was Sergt Draks 4 acs	08	00
vpl: 1 ac ½	01	10
2 oxen: 8 cows: 1 of 3 y	45	00
1 of 2 y: 1 of 1 y: 2 horfes		
4 fwine	15	00
	127	10

Samll Osborn

1 pfon	18	00
mead 7 acs yt was Jno Stiles	14	00
2 oxen: 2 cows 1 of 2 y		
1 horfe: 1 fwine	25	00
	57	00

John Owen

1 pfon	18	00
meadow 12 acs	22	00
vpl: 6 acs	06	00
2 oxen 3 cows 1 of 1 y	23	00
2 horfes 3 fwine	11	00
	80	00

Nathll Owin

1 pfone 1 horfe	22	00

John Porter Senir		
3 ꝑsons	54	00
housland 7 acs	08	00
in plimoth mead 15 acs ½	37	00
swamp 3 acs	03	00
East ye River 16 acs ½ meadow	39	00
4 horses: 1 of 2 y 2 oxen	28	00
6 cows: 2 of 3 y: 2 of 2 y		
1 of 1 y: 5 swine	40	00
	209	00

John Porter Junir		
3 ꝑsons	54	00
meadow 11 acs	21	00
7 acs mead of his fathers	13	00
2 acs vpl	02	00
3 horses: 1 of 1 y 2 oxen	23	00
6 cows: 3 of 3 y: 9 swine	42	00
	155	00

James Porter		
1 ꝑsone	18	00
mead 9 acs ½	18	00
3 horses 2 oxen 2 cows	30	00
1 of 2 y: 2 of 1 y: 7 swine	05	00
	71	00

Samll Pinny		
2 ꝑsons	36	00
8 acs ¾ marsh	06	00

house land 1 acre	01	00
East ye River 4 acs ½ mead	10	00
2 oxen: 2 cows: 1 of 2 y	20	00
1 of 1 y: 2 horſes 1 of 1 y		
4 ſwine	14	00
	87	00

Jno Pinny

1 ꝑſone	18	00
Eaſt ye river 9 acs ½ mead	20	00
3 oxen: 2 cows 2 horſes	31	00
	69	00

Iſaak Pinny

1 ꝑſone	18	00
houſe land 6 acs	07	00
in great mead 16 acs ½	39	00
2 oxen: 1 cow: 1 horſe	18	00
	82	00

Widw Pinny

1 ꝑſone	18	00
vpl: 13 acs	11	00
mead 28 acs	54	00
2 horſes: 1 oxe 3 cows	25	00
1 of 3 y: 2 of 2 y 5 ſwine	12	00
	120	00

Timo: Phelps Junir

1 ꝑſone 1 horſe	22	00

Wm Phelps		
1 pſone 2 horſes 1 oxe		
1 ac ½ upl:	33	00

Ephr̄ Phelps		
1 pſone 1 horſe: 1 of 2 y	24	00

Sergt Timo: Phelps		
4 pſons	72	00
houſe land 4 acs	04	00
mead 19 acs & 2 acs	46	00
vpl: 6 acs	05	00
2 horſes: 1 of 2 y: 2 oxen	20	00
4 cows: 2 of 1 y 4 ſwine	24	00
1 of 2 y 1 horſe	04	00
	175	00

Abraham Phelps		
2 pſons	36	00
houſe land 3 acs ½	03	15
meadow: 14 acs ½	33	00
5 acs mead eaſt river yt was A R	09	10
2 oxen: 5 cows: 2 of 4 y	38	00
1 of 2 y: 2 horſes 1 of 3 y		
2 of 2 y: 1 of 1 y & 6 ſwine	24	00
	144	05

John Phelps		
8 acs vpl	08	00
1 pſone: 1 ac houſe land	19	00

2 cows: 1 of 3 y: 1 of 2 y		
1 horſe 1 ſwine	18	00
	45	00
Joſeph Phelps		
1 pſone	18	00
vpl 26 acs	26	00
mead 20 acs	45	00
4 horſes 1 of 2 y: 2 oxen	28	00
2 cows: 2 of 2 y: 2 ſwine	14	00
	131	00
Timothy Palmer		
1 pſone	18	00
vpl: 6 acs: mead 1 ac	08	00
5 acs mead	10	00
2 horſes 2 oxen 3 cows	30	00
1 of 2 y: 4 ſwine	06	00
	72	00
Humph Prior[1]		
Timo Palmer Junir		
1 pſone 1 horſe	22	00
John Prior		
1 pſone 1 horſe	22	00
vpl: 5 acs: mead 2 acs	09	00
	31	00

1 This entry is crossed out.

Abrã Randoll

1 ꝑſone	18	00
houſe land 5 acs	05	00
In greate mead: 4 acs ½	11	00
2 cows: 1 horſe 2 ſwine	14	00
	48	00

Samll Rockwell

2 ꝑſones	36	00
more 1 ꝑſone	18	00
mead 2 acs ¼	05	00
vplnd 16 acs	16	00
land yt was Jno Rockwels	12	00
2 horſes 2 of 3 y: 1 of 2 y 1 of 1 y	17	00
2 oxen 2 cows 3 of 1 y		
2 ſwine	23	00
	127	00

Thos Rowlye

1 ꝑſone	18	00
mead 4 acs	08	00
2 cows: 1 of 1 y 1 ſwine	10	00
	36	00

Mrs Stoughton

2 ꝑſons	36	00
houſe land 11 acs	12	00
meadow 25 acs	58	00
vpl: & ſwamp 20 acs	20	00
2 oxen: 4 çows: 3 of 3 y	35	00

2 of 2 y: 2 of 1 y: 2 horfes		
1 fwine	15	00
	176	00

John Stoughton

1 pfone	18	00
mead 7 acs ½ vpland 4 acs	21	00
in greate mead 2 acs	04	10
2 horfes: 1 oxe: 4 cows		
1 of 2 y 1 fwine	32	00
	75	10

Thos Stoughton

1 pfone	18	00
meadw 7 acs ½: vpl 4 acs	21	00
in greate mead 2 acs	04	00
4 horfes	16	00
	59	00

Ens: Georg Sanders

1 pfone	18	00
vpl: 17 acs ½	20	00
2 horfes	08	00
	46	00

Jno Strong

2 pfons	36	00
houfeland 1 ac ¼	01	10
in greate mead 9 acs ¼	21	10
Eaft ye River mead 3 acs vland 18 acs	25	00

vpl: 4 acs	04	00
3 oxen 2 cows: 2 of 3 y	29	00
3 of 1 y: 4 horses 2 swine	21	00
	138	00

Corpll Return Strong

2 psons	36	00
houseland 2 acs	02	10
In greate mead 23 acs ½	49	10
in litle mead 2 acs ¼	05	00
To his pt in ye mill	17	00
To his pt in mr Warhams house land	18	00
1 oxe 1 of 4 y: 4 cows	25	00
3 of 2 y: 1 of 1 y 2 horses 1 of 2 y: 1 of 1 y 5 swine	23	00
	176	00

Nichos Senchion

1 psone	18	00
housel: 4 acs: vpl: 5 acs	08	00
mead 6 acs	13	00
1 horse 3 cows 2 swine	18	00
	57	00

Joseph Skinner

1 psone	18	00
housel: 2 acs	02	00
mead 4 acs ½	10	00
4 acs upl:	04	00

1 horſe 1 of 3 y 2 oxen	17	00
2 cows 1 of 3 y: 3 ſwine	14	00
	65	00

Wid^w Share

houſel: 5 ac^s	05	00
2 cows	08	00
	13	00

John Share

2 pſons	36	00
1 horſe	04	00
	40	00

Wid^w Stiles

houſel: 7 ac^s	07	00
mead 9 ac^s	17	00
2 cows 1 of 2 y	10	00
	34	00

Henry Stiles Seni^r

1 pſone	18	00
houſel: 2 ac^s	02	00
mead 4 ac^s	09	00
3 cows: 1 horſe: 1 ſwine	17	00
	46	00

Henry Stiles Juni^r

1 pſone: 1 horſe	22	00

John Stiles Estate

mead 7 ac^s	14	00[1]

This placed to S Osborn

1 The 14 is crossed out.

Robert Stedman

1 pſone	18	00
1 cow: 1 of 2 y: 2 ſwine	08	00
	26	00

Sanfords land 9 acs	18	00

John Saxton houſel: 2 acs	02	00

Owin Tudor Senir

houſel ¾ ac	01	00
mead 20 acs	46	00
at dearfeild 11 acs	11	00
5 horſes 2 oxen: 2 of 3 y 4 cows 1 of 1 y: 11 ſwine	64	00
	122	00

Owin Tudor Junir

2 horſes 1 pſone	26	00

Samll Tudor

1 pſone	18	00
1 ac houſe land	01	00
2 acs vpl: eaſt ye River	02	00
1 horſe 3 cows 2 of 3 y 1 of 1 y: 2 ſwine	25	00
	46	00

mr Stodder

his pt in ye mill	17	00

Timothy Trall Seni^{r}

1 ꝑſone	18	00
houſe la: 4 ac^{s}	05	00
mead 6 ac^{s} ½	15	00
at Hoyts mead 25 ac^{s}	52	00
vpl: & paſture 5 ac^{s}	04	00
2 oxen 4 cows: 2 of 2 y	30	00
1 of 1 y: 4 horſes	17	00
	141	00

Timo: Trall Juni^{r}

1 ꝑſone	18	00
in greate mead 3 ac^{s}	07	00
at 4th mead 2 ac^{s}	02	00
1 horſe 1 of 3 y	07	00
	34	00

Micah Tayntor

2 ꝑſons	36	00
houſela: 10 ac^{s}	10	00
at hoyts mead: 2 ac^{s} ½	05	00
houſel: 8 ac^{s}	08	00
2 cows 1 of 3 y 1 horſe	15	00
	74	00

Stephen Taylor Seni^{r}

1 ꝑſone	18	00
vpl: 26 ac^{s}	26	00
mead 14 ac^{s}	34	00
6 ſwine	06	00
	84	00

Stephen Taylor Junir

1 pſone	18	00
1 horſe 2 oxen 2 cows	22	00
1 of 2 y 2 of 1 y	04	00
2 cows: 2 of 2 y: 2 of 1 y 4 ſwine	18	00
	62	00

Mr Simon Wolcot

3 pſons	54	00
mead: 57 acs	123	00
1 ac vpl	01	00
2 horſes 2 oxen 3 cows	30	00
1 of 3 y: 1 of 2 y: 1 ſwine	06	00
	214	00

Henry Wolcot

2 pſons	36	00
houſel: & paſtr 14 acs	16	00
meadow 50 acs	107	00
2 acs upl: 5½ acs mead yt was mr Chauncies	013	00
3 oxen 9 cows 2 of 2 y	055	00
2 horſes 3 of 1 y: 11 ſwine	023	00
	250	00

Mr John Wolcot

houſe land 19 ac	22	00
1 perſone	18	00
mead 24 acs	55	00
East ye River 32 acs mead	70	14
vpl: 19 acs	16	06

at Hartf: ſwamp 3 ac^s	03	00
2 horſes 2 oxen 4 cows	34	00
3 of 3 y: 1 of 2 y		
3 of 1 y 5 ſwine	19	00
	238	00

Robert Watſon

5 ac^s vpl: at ſtony brook	05	00
4 ꝑſons	72	00
houſeland 15 ac^s	17	00
mead 7 ac^s	16	00
Eaſt river 14 ac^s	31	00
4 oxen 6 cows 4 of 3 y	56	00
2 of 2 [ ] of 1 y: 3 horſes		
1 of 3 y: 9 ſwine	32	00
	229	00

Ebenez: Watſon

1 ꝑſone 1 horſe	22	00

Nath^{ll} Watſon

1 ꝑſone	18	00

Nath^{ll} Winchell

2 ꝑſons	36	00
houſeland 12 ac^s	12	00
mead: 10 ac^s	21	00
East ye River 8 ac^s	17	00
2 oxen 4 cows: 2 of 2 y	30	00

4 of 1 y: 2 horſes		
1 of 1 y: 1 ſwine	15	00
	131	00
Nath^ll^ Winchell Juni^r^		
1 pſone removed	x 18	00
Sam^ll^ Wilſon		
1 pſone	18	00
houſel 3 ac^s^	03	00
mead 2 ac^s^	04	00
1 horſe 1 cow 5 ſwine	13	00
	38	00
Jno Williams		
	18	00
2 pſones & Iſack Eglestons pſon	18	00
houſe land 16 ac^s^	18	00
houſe land of his wifes	01	00
5 ac^s^ mead y^t^ was I Egleſtons	11	00
2 oxen 1 cow 2 ſwine	16	00
	82	00
4 ac^s^ vpland y^t^ was Tahans	04	00
	86	00
Francis Sydinham		
1 pſone & trade	60	00
Thos Kelſie		
1 pſone	18	00

Danll Willet			
1 pſone 1 horſe		22	00
Thos Biſhop[1]			
1 pſone[1] remooved			
Benj: Bartlet			
1 pſone		18	00
Jehoj: Bartlet			
1 pſone		18	00
Thos Browne			
1 pſone remooued	x	18	00
Benj: Banes			
1 pſone		18	00
Danll Garret[1]			
4 acs ½ meadow	x	10[1]	00
Joſhua Willis			
Eaſt ye River 8 acs		08	00
1 hors: 2 cows: 1 of 1 y.		13	00
1 pſone		18	00
		39	00
Samll Brooks			
1 pſone[1]		18	00[1]

1 Crossed out.

Willm Peire
1 ꝑſone 18 00

John Sparke
1 ꝑſone 18 00

Iſack Thayre
1 ꝑſone 18 00

Eleazer Gaylor
1 ꝑſone 18 00

Thos Pope
1 horſe 1 ꝑſone 22 00

Sam^{ll} Church
1 ꝑſoue 18 00

William Simpſon
1 ꝑſone 18 00

Robert Lake
1 ꝑſone 18 00

15260-06
Persons 270

Edmund Marſhall
1 ꝑſone 18 00

3 oxen: 3 cows: 1 of 1 y 2 horfes	36	00
	54	00

John Huggin

1 ꝑfone	18	00
1 horfe 1 cow	08	00
	26	00

John Mihill

3 ꝑfons	54	00
1 horfe 1 oxe 2 cows 1 of 3 y:	20	00
	74	00

Richard Woollery

1 ꝑfone	18	00
1 horfe 2 cows 1 of 3 y 1 of 1 y:	16	00
	34	00

Thos Stephens

1 ꝑfone	18	00
1 horfe 2 cowes	12	00
	30	00

perfons 277

Summa	1547l	06s

By us Jacob drake
John ffyler
Samuel Grante
James Enno

Examined & aprooued by us
John Moffe
Wm Dudley

[Endorsed] Windſo^r List 1686

APPENDIX

TO

MATTHEW GRANT RECORD

(See page III)

Page 22, for line 19 read

Georg Allixander married ſuſan . march . 18 . 1[644]

Page 22, for line 25 read

Thomas Allyn marryed Abigayl warram . october . [1658]

Page 24, for line 15 read

Nathanell Biſsell . maried mindwell moors . ſeptm[r] . 25 . [1662]

Page 25, for line 4 read

John . Barber maried Bathſheba cogens . ſeptm[r] . [2 . 1663]

Page 25, for line 7 read

Thomas Barber married mary Phelps . Dece[mb[r] . 17 . 1663]

Page 25, for line 8 read [Barber family]

his Daughtr marcy was Borne . Janury . 11 . 6[6]

Page 25, for line 10 read

Samuell Barber married mary cogens . [Decm[r] . ye 1 . 1670]

Page 28, for line 8 read

Beniamen Bartlet married . Debra Barnard . Ju[ly 1664]

Page 35, for line 20 read
[Mar]y eleſworth was Borne . may . 7 . 1660

Page 35, for line 25 read
Job ſonn of Joſias eleſwort was born . Aprel . 13 . 167[4]

Page 36, for line 4 read
his Daughter Heſter egelſton was borne . decm[r] . 1 . 166[3]

Page 36, for line 17 read
his ſonn John ſillar borne . ye 2 . baptiſed ye . 11 . 16[76]

Page 36, for line 19 read
ff William ſilly and margret his wif ware married . ſeptem[r] . 2 . 164[2]

Page 37, for line 20 read
[Samuel] of ſamuell forward was Borne . July . 23 . 1671 .

Page 37, for line 21 read
[Joseph] of ſamuell forward was Borne . noumb . 10 . 1674 .

Page 38, for line 22 read
his ſonn John Grant was Borne . octobr . 20 . 167[0]

Page 38, for line 23 read [*Grant family*]
his Daughter mary was Borne . Aprell . 26 . 16[75]

Page 39, for line 15 read [*Gillet family*]
dyed Ju[ne] 11

Page 40, for line 9 read
[John Gille]t married marcy Barber . July . 8 . 1669 .

Page 41, for line 13 read
georg Grifwold married mary Holcom . octobr . 3 . [165]

Page 41, for line 15 read
his fonn Thomas grifwold was Borne . feptem^r^ . 29 . 165[8]

Page 44, for line 1 read [Gibbs family]
his Daughter [Elizabeth[1]] born feptem^r^ . 13 . 16[7]

Page 45, for line 17 read
his fonn Nathanell Hofford was Born . aguft [. 19 . 1671]

Page 45, for line 19 read
obadia fonn of John Hofford was born feptmb [20] . 167[ ]

Page 48, for line 18 read [Loomis family]
his Daughter mary was Borne . Auguft . 7 . 1673 . Dead may . 14 . 7[4]

Page 50, for line 18 read [Chauncey family]
his daughter Abigayl was born october ye 14 . 16[77] that

Page 52, line 5 should read [Moses family]
his Daughter margret born . Decembr . 2 . 1666 .

1 Parts of some of the letters in this word can still be seen. It does not seem possible that the name could have been Elizabeth.

Page 52, for line 12 read [Moore family]
his Daughter fara was Borne . Defembr . 6 . [167]

Page 56, for line 19 read [Phelps family]
And he marryed a . 2 . frances ye wido of Thomas Dewey . noumbr [2] 164[8]

Page 63, line 12 has also been copied [Rockwell family]
his fonn John he had by hir was Borne feptem^r 6 . 1663 . Dyed

Page 65, for line 6 read
Richard Saxfton marryed . fara Cook . Aprell . 16 . 164[6]

Page 67, line 10 has also been copied
Peter Tilton married his wife elifabeth . may . 10 . 1639

Page 67, for line 11 read [Tilton family .]
his Daughter elifabeth was Borne . Juen . baptifed . 19 Day . 16[40]

Page 68, for line 13 read
owen Tudor marryed mary fkiner wido . noum^r . 13 . 16[51]

Page 68, for line 14 read [Tudor family]
his fonn famuel and Daughter fara born both at a berth . noum^r . 26 . 16[52]

Page 68, for line 24 read [Warham family]
his wife Jane dyed . at norwake Aprel [2]3 . 16[4]5 .

Page 70, for line 9 read

Richard weller married Ann Wilſon. ſeptm^{r} . 17. 16[40]

Page 73, for line 16 read [Hillyer family]

his dafter Ann was born may ye 8 . 1687[1] . and dyed . July . 17 . 8[7]

Page 77, for line 16 read

Danell ſon of John loomis maryed, maried mary Elezwo[rth]

---

1 This date was written 1677; but the third figure is blotted, perhaps by an endeavor to alter it to an 8, as some have read it.

INDEX

CPSIA information can be obtained
at www.ICGtesting.com
Printed in the USA
BVHW04*1207070818
523813BV00007B/73/P